INTERNATIONAL SERIES OF MONOGRAPHS ON
LIBRARY AND INFORMATION SCIENCE
GENERAL EDITOR: G. CHANDLER

VOLUME 1

BASES OF MODERN LIBRARIANSHIP

BASES OF MODERN LIBRARIANSHIP

A Study of Library Theory and Practice in Britain, Canada, Denmark, The Federal Republic of Germany and the United States

EDITED BY

CARL M. WHITE

*former Chair Professor of Library Science
and Director of the Institute of Librarianship
Faculty of Letters, University of Ankara*

PERGAMON PRESS

OXFORD · LONDON · EDINBURGH · NEW YORK
PARIS · FRANKFURT

1964

PERGAMON PRESS LTD.
Headington Hill Hall, Oxford
4 & 5 Fitzroy Square, London W.1

PERGAMON PRESS (SCOTLAND) LTD.
2 & 3 Teviot Place, Edinburgh 1

PERGAMON PRESS INC.
122 East 55th Street, New York 22, N.Y.

GAUTHIER-VILLARS ED.
55 Quai des Grands-Augustins, Paris 6

PERGAMON PRESS G.m.b.H.
Kaiserstrasse 75, Frankfurt am Main

Distributed in the Western Hemisphere by
THE MACMILLAN COMPANY · NEW YORK
persuant to a special arrangement with
Pergamon Press Limited

Library of Congress Catalog Card Number 64-12831

Set in Monotype Baskerville 11 on 12 pt.
and printed in Great Britain by
T. & A. Constable Ltd., Hopetoun Street, Edinburgh

CONTENTS

v

CONTENTS

LIST OF PLATES

PREFACE

THE Faculty of Letters of Ankara University sponsored an International Series of Lectures on Librarianship during the academic year, 1960–61. The lecturers were librarians of international standing who had been selected by their Governments, the Federal Republic of Germany, Great Britain and the United States of America. Canada and Denmark were unable to send lecturers to Ankara but participated by contributing papers. This volume is made up of contributions from these four sources plus two other chapters which were prepared to round out the treatment. Short introductions by presiding officers are included, not only for their ideas on books and libraries but also for biographical information about the panel of contributors.

Turkey's first, and to date her only, degree program in library science was established in the Faculty of Letters in 1954–55. There were several problems to cope with. One was development of the literature. Students and practitioners needed to draw upon experience elsewhere but found the material in no one language entirely satisfactory for the purpose. The trouble lay partly in the fact that the foreign language known by one person was not understood by enough of his colleagues for the literature in it to be used by all of them; but it went deeper than language. The findings of a physicist have universal application, but this of course is not always true in the social sciences including library science. Conclusions about economic conditions or literacy or political behavior in—for example—Sweden, China or South Africa may, elsewhere, have quite limited application. The trouble with library literature lay in this matter of ready applicability. While certain countries have had experience in handling libraries so valuable that developing nations like Turkey could neglect it only to their disadvantage, treatises which summarize this experience for ready adaptation to alien conditions were found to be scarce. The present work originated to help fill this gap.

An English edition is published in the belief that a work which serves one developing country may be of some value to others. Like the Turkish original, this edition is addressed in the first instance to students and practising librarians; but it contains information which will aid scholars, Government officials and all public-spirited citizens who have the interests of good library service at heart. Just as water seeks its own level, so the library achievements of any nation tend to rise to the level of its leaders' expectations, and no higher. Here are materials to use in deciding on the kind of library program a nation expects to have.

The comparative study in Chapter 2 is based mainly on the three library systems which are treated most fully in later chapters.

Experience indicates that success in organizing and administering libraries in some countries is seriously hampered by failure to take account of differences between personal libraries (or libraries where analagous practices prevail) and those libraries which are maintained at public expense for the use of the public. To assist in discussing problems which grow out of confusing the two groups, some attention is given to ways in which they differ.

The object of this slender volume is hardly that of adding to the existing fund of knowledge about librarianship. It is more a primer of library thought where the object is to gather up and systematize knowledge that has been a long time in the making. If the contributors succeed in laying hold of essentials of librarianship in these four countries, they are entitled to rather more credit than would be the case if the field were older and the lines along which they have worked, already laid out. The achieving of synthesis in many fields requires a writer merely to bring some earlier work up to date. These contributors had no such models to guide them.

It is not possible to thank each of the many persons who joined in seeing that the Series did its work. They include officials of cooperating Governments, the Minister of Education, the Rector of the University, the Dean and the Faculty of Letters, the entire staff of the Chair of Library Science, the student body and Ankara librarians. Grateful acknowledgement is made to all of these. Their labors received recognition in one form that was not anticipated. As the Series progressed, attention was drawn to the fact that the method—while not new—has wider application. Experts from different nations pooled their experience. They came one at a time, permitting them to be of service for two weeks outside the lecture hall in small group meetings and private conferences. Foreign nations aided but did not lose their identity in the process. Those who shared in the work commend the procedure to others who in coping with local problems need the benefit of international cooperation.

CARL M. WHITE

Ankara, Turkey

1. THE INTERTWINED DESTINY OF LITERATE SOCIETY AND LIBRARIANSHIP

CARL M. WHITE

INTEREST in educating librarians has been rapidly spreading since World War II. For example, "almost every library development project" submitted to UNESCO in recent years has included a request in some form for aid in library training. UNESCO has responded with fellowships, with temporary training programs and the advice that "The fundamental problem of training professional librarians is one which has to be faced nationally by the creation of good national schools".

Older and younger nations agree. Britain, Canada, Germany, India and the U.S.A. are prominent among those which have well-established library schools. Russia made a late start but is pushing the work with much vigor. Cuba, Iran, Israel, Japan and Turkey have all organized programs since the War.

Men have known libraries for centuries, but there are men still living who were born before the first library school was established in the 1880's. Here and there this wide gap in age is taken to mean that libraries can in the future as in the past get along without education for librarians; that current interest in the latter is perhaps more a fashion than a necessity.

The university education of librarians derives significance from encouraging inquiry that goes deeper than uncritical explanations of this kind. The thesis advanced in this chapter is that the connection between modern librarianship and modern civilization is close enough to make educated librarians more or less indispensable. The object of the discussion to follow is to show what the interconnection is.

Writings on library history tend to describe individual libraries or the libraries of a country or period. These accounts can be expected to cover such topics as: the growth of collections, acquisitions, classification and cataloging, housing, financing, regulations and personnel. All of this information is good as far as it goes, but too often it leaves the reader to search in vain among assorted facts for some internal order—some mosaic—which will give the several fragments range of meaning. It is of course plain to all that libraries are among the things that are products of human effort, so if some larger configuration of meaning is to be found in their history, it is better to relate them to the whole stream of social evolution than to separate them as it were from human strivings. What

I

has man been striving to do which accounts for his having a history of libraries at all?

While there is too much backwardness in library development for the present generation in any country to feel complacent about it, modern library achievements in the aggregate are undoubtedly beyond anything that could have been imagined back when it all began. To get from there to here, man had no lodestar to guide him along a predetermined course; he had to try and fail and start again. Across the centuries countless footsteps gradually beat into shape a few giant strides forward. It is these achievements, not a chronicling of activities internal to some library system or period, which form the more significant chapters of the epic.

START OF A REVOLUTION IN THE COMMUNICATION AND RECORDING OF IDEAS

The first long stride was the act of developing an instrument which empowers one mind to reach across all barriers of space and time and communicate a message to other minds. The feat involved inventing writing, experimenting with different kinds of writing material and testing the merits of the tablet and scroll against the merits of the codex. Ancient bookmen of Bergama contributed a writing material, parchment, whose superiority over clay tablets and papyrus hastened the forming of the book as we know it. It was a step that took centuries, but the work was done so well that the physical form of the book has in essential respects remained the same ever since. In range of influence, none of man's other achievements surpasses the invention of writing and the book. All those who live in the crescent which bounds the Eastern Mediterranean are entitled to undying pride in it.

PRIVATE LIBRARIES

But we are getting ahead of the story. To speak of the influence of the new instrument is to go a long way past the invention of letters *per se*, on past the triumph of the codex to the social effects of the revolution they brought about. To picture the second step something needs to be said about the evolution of the use of letters.

Writing found a variety of uses ranging from keeping accounts to publishing official news or transmitting short messages of lesser importance. Early thinkers however turned the use of the new medium away from simple recording or publicizing events and names to the presentation of sustained sequences of thought. It was writing in this form that men took to their hearts enough to make them start building collections.

When in the dim past this practice of collecting the writings of others began, the library idea was born.

Library collections to start with were private. "Private libraries" will be used here to include not only those libraries which are owned by and serve a person or family but also those organization libraries which are administered along lines similar to personal libraries, whether their doors are ajar to outsiders or not. The creation of the private library was the second step forward. It has an institutional pattern which is characteristic, influential, yet not commonly noticed since it shades so imperceptibly into a later pattern—that of the library which is organized to further the interests of the public. To start with, the sponsor of the private library was and normally still is the source of financial support, the governing authority, clientele ("public" served) and library staff all rolled into one.

In this characterization, nothing is said of the purpose of the private library. The subject is a complex one, for books have a many-sided appeal. What for example did Willibald Perkheimer of Nuremberg mean by announcing on his bookplate that his superb collection of 2000 volumes was for himself and his friends (sibi et amicis)? The answer in part is suggested by Nicholas V when he speaks of a certain inexplicable thirst for books (certe inesplicabile sete di libri) which drove him on to notable success in building the Vatican collection. How many private collectors, like him, have built their libraries because of a love for books and a desire to be near them! Great calligraphers, scribes and typographers have all shared this devotion with great collectors.

Caesar helped to popularize motives of another sort by bringing home captive libraries as trophies of war. Roman patricians, aided by a flourishing booktrade, started building collections of their own. It became so fashionable that Seneca once wryly observed that things had got to the point where a library was considered, along with hot and cold baths, as necessary adornment for a home: "Iam enim inter balnearia et thermas bibliotheca quoque ut necessarium domus ornamentum expolitur." Time passed, and as wealth increased merchant princes adopted the habits of collecting books as symbols of status, while the example of those rulers who were genuinely interested in learning was followed by others who collected with equal zeal mainly to add lustre to their courts.

The ultimate benefit to civilization from collecting books shows no consistent relation to the motives of collectors, but it has been pointed out time and again from Seneca and the humanists down to the present that the many uses which are made of books for purposes other than reading and study are all derivative ones. Man started building libraries in order to hold concourse with other thinkers and something happened to him in the process. He grew in stature; his life was enriched; and in some ways he was made over into a new man. The private library is here identified as the second step in the advance towards the twentieth century because of this influence which it has exerted in the making of civilized man. In the heyday of its influence, it had an effectiveness which has in some particulars never been matched by its institutional successor, the library organized to serve the general public: until as late as the eighteenth century, a man was able to surround himself in one room with the total record of learning, or at least all of it he had need for. The specialization of knowledge since then, coupled with other changes, has gradually forced the library built around the interests of one man into a subordinate place, and the intellectual worker in consequence finds himself dependent on libraries which are larger, more complex and farther away from his own study. It leaves a feeling of nostalgia. Who does not long at times for a recovery of this older standard of service which puts within arm's reach all the books a man ever needs?

RISE OF SOCIETY BASED ON LETTERS AND LEARNING

This is the step that lies between dependence on private libraries and the rise of libraries organized to serve needs of a different magnitude.

There is precedent for using "preliterate" or "non-literate" to refer to a culture where little or no use is made of letters. "Literate society" will be used in a similar manner here to refer to a culture with a built-in need for letters—or, to be more technical, to refer to a culture which depends so heavily on books, reading and writing for recording and communicating ideas that letters may be deemed indispensable to its good health and indeed its very survival. Societies still exist that are predominately non-literate while, on the other hand, islands of non-literates or semi-literates are to be found in all literate societies. This however should not be allowed to obscure the fact that Western man has since the Renaissance developed societies where the use of letters is inseparable from matters which are essential to keeping people who are now the most advanced from sliding back to a lower state of civilization. Common speech takes this for granted and makes the use of letters a rough equivalent of the sort of learning which is indicative of the highest civilization.

Modern civilization wherever it comes into full bloom seems invariably to be preceded by the birth or rebirth of the humanistic spirit. This remarkable force eludes definition but is associated with a regard for the dignity of human personality, an intrepid challenging of arbitrary authority, a resolute faith in the ability of emancipated minds to find their way to truth and noble destiny. In the West, the building of modern civilization has meant the slow weaving of a fabric of human institutions which are embodiments of the humanistic spirit, and here are some examples:

The rise of the great freedoms of inquiry, speech and conscience.

The organization of formal schooling, the curbing of labor practices which interfere with prolonged, systematic education of children, the spread of required attendance at school as a means of preparing youth for their adult responsibilities.

The rise of universities, the rise of enlightened patronage of letters and learning by individuals, private organizations and the state, the growth of public support for systematic pursuit and dissemination of knowledge.

The invention of printing, organization of prosperous trade in books, maintenance of high professional standards among publishers and booksellers.

Displacement of guild-control over "useful knowledge", recognition of copyright and other rights of patent.

Acceptance of the rule of law and the attendant growth of parliamentary systems, a step which made written codes essential to the processes of government.

Spread of universal suffrage, which hinged the future of self-government on the enlightenment of the individual citizen.

Development of the newspaper, popular magazine and other media to aid in the diffusion of knowledge and informed opinion.

Decline of the monastic ideal of scholarship, progressive acceptance by men of letters and learning of responsibility for imparting knowledge and information through written channels, the rise of entirely new professions such as journalists and librarians to aid in closing the gap between rapid advances in knowledge and the application of knowledge in social practice.

Recognition of the dignity of work, decline of the concept of learning as the prerogative of a ruling class separate from the workers, reconstruction of higher education as a deliberate aid to developing leaders in all those fields having an intellectual base which are required for the good of a society of workers.

The last named item, it is worth adding, was an answer given by liberal people years before international communism rose to make its own peculiar challenge to education based on class distinctions.

The list of civilized advances enumerated above do not of themselves prove that habitual exercise of freedom of expression or reliance on written codes of behavior, etc., builds dependence on letters into the fundamental processes of modern civilization. The proposition can be presented with more cogency by taking a particular advance such as the industrial revolution and showing what the interconnection is. Any relation which the industrial revolution may have to twentieth century needs for library service may not be as transparent as other examples that might be chosen, but it is of course fitting to use just such an example in searching for proof.

In a narrow sense, the industrial revolution was an episode that is now entirely past—a switch to the factory system following the introduction of power-driven machinery to replace hand-labor, after 1760. It enabled England to forge ahead in all lines where the new source of power could be put to work. In an effort to keep pace, other nations struck back in what Bismarck called a new kind of war which was to pit the technical competence of one nation against that of another. France concentrated on products requiring good taste and superior craftsmanship. The results shown in the early international expositions, which began with the one in the Crystal Palace in London in 1851, were considered by a good many observers as proof of inborn superiority of French workmen. A German study however brought out the fact that the superiority lay rather in the type of training the craftsmen were receiving. To skip over absorbing details in order to bring the story down to date, the rivalry shifted from public expositions to training establishments, scientific laboratories, libraries of information, and there it remains. The lesson is now commonplace knowledge: the economic capability of a nation depends on access to raw materials, access to better knowledge than one's competitor, and well-qualified manpower.

In other words, while the application of power-driven machinery to production was one episode in one country, it was at the same time a spectacular inauguration of a process that has spread to many countries and is still spreading. It is the habit, both social and personal, of applying to the business of everyday life the best ideas—or to use another phrase, the best intelligence—available from the recorded experience of the race as a whole.

The significance of this habit in revolutionizing industry and in devising other ways of doing things can best be seen by contrasting it with the habit of depending on tradition. The dependence on handed-down ways is not met so often in countries where habits of thought engendered by the industrial revolution have made themselves felt, but no country is free from it. For example, at the southern tip of one of America's loveliest mountain ranges nestles the little town of Andrews, North Carolina. Years ago, Andrews prospered from making tannic acid out of the bark of the chestnut tree. Then somewhere beyond this secluded valley improvements in producing tannic acid were introduced. Andrews failed to keep up. Hard times fell on the people, and the prosperity they lost has not been regained. The lesson is the same for men everywhere: ways handed down from the past are not always the best, yet they often hold people back from free application of new-found knowledge in daily life. Those who would make such application, wherever they are, find it imperative to have at hand the books, journals and other sources through which knowledge is disseminated.

The foregoing focusses attention on the organized practice of using the best available information to promote material progress. To give balance to the treatment, it should be stressed that modern society shows even greater organized dependence on letters in intellectual and spiritual matters. The point can be illustrated by referring briefly to the rise of the university, one of the most original institutions to be perfected by literate society. It is impossible to point to a date and say, "This is when the university originated"; but in terms of the sociology of learning, the essential pre-condition of its rise was an accumulated intellectual heritage voluminous enough to justify splitting off a new division of labor and turning it over to specialists called professors who were ready to devote their energies to its transmission and further development. Not enough is known about the steps which led up to this departure. One of the extraordinary things about it is that while the university movement has been predominantly secular, the adherents of no less than three great religions figured in originating it. Further search of manuscripts scattered around the southerly crescent extending from the Bosphorus to Gibraltar will undoubtedly throw further light on these contacts. Already however enough is known to say that between the fifth and the twelfth century Western man was finding it increasingly difficult to educate youth by continuing to rely on the preliterate methods of live memory and the spoken word. Unheard of in preliterate society, the university arose to cultivate youth and higher learning in a society which was making ever wider use of letters, and in time it obviously further widened the gap between the two worlds.

The superior achievements which set the two worlds apart—the world created by literate peoples and the world created by non-literate peoples —have now and then been attributed to differences of native intelligence. Anthropologists find no support for this idea that one race or people has innate intellectual capabilities denied others. Their findings however do establish a close connection between superiority in civilized arts on one hand and skill in accumulating and using man's intellectual heritage on the other. The library is the chief instrument so far perfected for the performance of this latter function, and its claim to indispensability in literate society can be indicated by elaborating briefly the idea just stated.

By learning to depend on letters instead of depending merely on live memory and the spoken word, man vastly increased his effectiveness in

B

preparing youth for adulthood. Since the library has been perfected as the principal vehicle for carrying forward and making available the intellectual resources that need to be accumulated for use, this statement means for one thing that formal education at all levels can be conducted more effectively with well-equipped libraries. There are few left today who would dispute this: community after community the world over is struggling to adopt and maintain high library standards as a means of improving schools, colleges and universities. The central point, however, goes far beyond what this community or that may or may not wish to do. Assume two cultures where native ability is the same but one is literate and the other is preliterate. The educational capabilities of the two people in such a case will necessarily differ, regardless of what the community is innately capable of, or wishes to do. One will be capable of prolonged, systematic education and will confer degrees signifying high intellectual accomplishment, but the other will not. Man in other words is incapable of prolonged, systematic education of youth in subjects of great erudition except as normal capability is spliced by that social facility which has come to be known as the library.

THE REMAKING OF LIBRARIANSHIP

Collecting the thought of others had to wait as was seen till the use of letters to convey thought was perfected. Similarly, modern librarianship had to wait on the creation of a society where man's need for intellectual sources was so great that private libraries could no longer meet the demands by themselves. The fourth and last step to be noted was the movement to develop library service on a scale commensurate with these demands, and the rest of the book shows how representative nations have gone about it. National programs differ, as one might expect of separate creations of energetic peoples faced each with its own peculiar conditions. Major library systems of the world nevertheless have enough in common to set modern librarianship off as a stage noticeably different from the past.

Librarianship as portrayed in the chapters to follow is not very old. Ernst Cassirer describes Leibniz (1646–1716) as the last man of learning to master the total sum of recorded thought. Limits were being reached beyond which the mind could not keep up with or fully utilize the learning that was accumulating without relying upon the specialty which the library profession was to rise to handle. It is plain in retrospect to see what librarians of a new type were needed for. It was up to somebody to assemble, organize and make available this expanding record of the mind. It could no longer be done by private individuals who took on the responsibility as a side job while doing other things. To develop this emerging specialty in scale with the times, library service would have to be organized and supported along the lines of other public responsibilities like police protection, formal schooling, and public health. High standards of service would be required for all classes of people, of all ages, and steady financing in terms of program needs would be called for.

Librarians as late as the eighteenth century, at the time of Leibniz, were clearly not ready for this responsibility. The chaotic state then of library organization and service is described in Zachrias K. von Uffenbach's *Merkwürdige Reisen durch Niedersachsen*. Uffenbach shows a clear grasp of the way any undertaking depends for success on the calibre of people who are in charge of it, but blames library personnel to a degree that suggests insensitiveness to the role others besides the specialists play in the launching of a profession. What Uffenbach overlooks is that the act of instituting any new division of labor is a social act: it is not taken till the people who form the society will it. The social climate affects the rate at which the new movement advances, indeed whether it gets under way at all. Once under way, it is again the attitude of people outside the specialty that determines the social status, the economic incentives and other perquisites held out to those who choose to invest their lives in the work. The over-all social worth thus attached to the calling in turn has a reflex effect on whether superior or mediocre people are recruited. If leaders of the eighteenth century society cannot be absolved from their share of responsibility for the mediocre library talent recruited, neither can they be excused for the state of morale among library workers. The people of an emergent calling, just as others, rise to the full height of their powers with greater heart when the work they pour their lives into is treated with respect. Library work had by the eighteenth century risen in dignity in some ways since the days when educated Greek slaves served the best Roman families in luxurious surroundings, but the disheartening conditions pictured by Uffenbach leave so little ground for professional pride that the librarians he criticizes may have wondered at times whether the advantages were all on their side.

The transition to the twentieth century owes much to enriched material and bibliographical resources, but even more to leaders inside and outside libraries who promoted a new concept of librarianship. One of these was Leibniz, who served for a while as librarian of Wölfbuttel. If he came toward the end of the line of men of universal learning, he was at the same time among the first to see that a world which was enlarging the record of the mind so rapidly was, in the process, developing built-in requirements for a library program well beyond the capabilities of the private library. His proposals for developing research libraries included: establishing a basis of support firm enough to assure continuous development of collections; regular appropriations; systematic acquisition of all

major works of outstanding contributors to learning; classification of
the entire collection; an alphabetical catalog, with subject index; the
entire administration to be aimed at giving the library a role in the life
of the state and society comparable in importance to that of the school
and the church. The remarkable progress of the Göttingen library in the
eighteenth century, other advances in and out of Germany inspired by
its example, even the spur to library development given by Althoff late
in the nineteenth century, all felt the influence of Leibniz' ideas. He
was however ahead of his time. In France, the Royal Library, already
of leading rank in his time, was undoubtedly the most princely library
in the world when the Revolution struck, yet it was more a national
treasure than an institution designed to serve the intellectual needs of
the public. Across the channel, the British Museum, with its library,
opened in 1759. It was to provide "free access to all studious and curious
persons" but the era of public service for which it became world famous
could hardly be said to have begun before the reforms which occurred
toward the middle of the nineteenth century. Hansard's *Debates* quotes
William Cobbett as saying of it in 1833: "Why should tradesmen and
farmers be called upon to pay for the support of a place which was intended only for the amusement of the curious and rich, and not for the
benefit or the instruction of the poor? If the aristocracy wanted the
Museum as a lounging place, let them pay for it."

THE EDUCATION OF LIBRARIANS

From all this emerges a simple conclusion about what man, the architect of twentieth century librarianship, has been striving to do. He has
been learning how to use letters more nearly to achieve his full potential
in the realms of mind and heart; learning how to build a civilization in
which he and these things he so highly prizes will be at home; and in so
doing, learning how to apply to the practical problems that beset him
the best fruits of the mind regardless of time or place of origin.

These past advances suggest asking what the next advance will be,
but this is a question which cannot be answered any more than one
could tell at the other end of library history what the future held. Present-
day uses of the image, the recapture through radio of the power of the
spoken word, recent break-through to mechanical storage and retrieval
of information, will undoubtedly affect the future of libraries: they are
already affecting the society to which libraries have become indigenous.
Whether the influence of the printed page, relative to these, is waxing or
waning is hardly the central point about the epic of literate society and
its libraries. Writing is only one means of communicating ideas. Its per-
fection was the first step, but only the first, in the course of developments

which have given man power to retain, organize and use the accumulated heritage of all generations of all mankind. If it is possible to single out one thing among many as a special preoccupation of modern librarianship, it would be fair to say its chief concern is to assure continuance and full use of this power. The future of a particular means of doing it, such as the printed page, is secondary to this larger purpose. One hastens to add that the newer media of mass communication, mechanical storage and retrieval of information, etc., appear so far to be rather supplements than substitutes for the book. To date, the latter has found no match as a means of communicating sustained sequences of thought across barriers of space and time.

This is the perspective which gives the tide of interest in educated librarians which is rising around the world its special meaning. Pushing from below are new forces and demands which make trained manpower in this field more important in more nations than ever before.

It may be asked why the responsibility for providing qualified library personnel is gravitating to universities. The answer falls into four parts. First, the library task of the race has grown to a magnitude where it challenges and rewards the best minds. This alone is enough to enkindle the interest of university men. Over hundreds of years, universities have steadily broadened their usefulness to the public. They have done so by making it their special task to develop leaders in all divisions of human endeavor which involve a high degree of intellectual cultivation. Second, universities are concerned about the future of their own libraries, and would be slow to accept librarians who are not university trained. Third, all leading nations have experimented with the use of apprenticeship in training librarians, only to find that this ancient method of instruction, while it has its uses in manual trades and occupations, is in the field of librarianship wasteful in money and time—wasteful above all of priceless assets of youth which are never regained once lost. It is on this account that recent library history in all major countries shows a slow but unmistakable drift away from apprenticeship towards methods of instruction which have been pioneered and perfected in centers of formal education.

Fourth, experience in educating librarians is still limited when compared with professions where curricula have been in operation for hundreds of years, but library science is rapidly gaining recognition as a field of study and research which not only commands the respect of university men but requires for the solution of its problems the same standards of scholarship applied in other fields. There is a rapidly-growing library literature which represents scholarship of a high order. Research in librarianship however is not yet highly developed, and it is important to understand that the reason lies in the way most nations start out. When thinkers in the practising arts have the freedom to do so, they normally set to work to develop through research a scientific base, a substructure of theory from which evolve changes in the arts themselves. The tendency is illustrated by the history of the emergence of medical research, research in jurisprudence, etc. The same tendency can be seen in those library schools where the teaching of beginners has ceased to be an all-consuming task. A case can be made for developing the research potential of a new field from the outset, but the characteristic procedure in most countries has been to begin the other way around and to concentrate at first on instructing young librarians to go out and take charge of practical library operations.

University sponsorship of the education of librarians has yielded two principal benefits. It has raised the level of scholarship, introduced research and research programs in a field where nothing of the sort had existed before. Second, it has broadened the education of the operating personnel, balancing instruction in the technology of the subject with supporting instruction in other fields. Libraries are concerned with the entire spectrum of knowledge: balanced instruction thus becomes of necessity an interdepartmental task. In this respect, educating librarians is something like educating writers. Each speciality, writing just as librarianship, presupposes a certain technical competence as well as a special language and some knowledge of a particular literature, all of which can be taught by a *single* department. But the great librarian, just as the great writer, needs that well-rounded intellectual development which normally is the contribution of several sister disciplines working together in unison. The prevailing philosophy of education for librarianship is quite specific in assuming, first, that the prime requisite of the well-qualified librarian is a university education and, second, that the function of a library school is one of rounding off a general university education with that more specialized preparation which is essential to intelligent practice of this profession.

Is the library the creature or the creator of this literate world in which we live and move and have our being? It is both at once. Librarianship stands for the accumulated power over the works of the mind, and our type of civilization depends on the works of the mind as the mammal depends on the heart-beat. Any civilization is always in process of change and ours in some ways magnifies change; but the changes we sanction are those sanctioned by reason, intelligence. Till such time therefore as man turns back the clock towards dependence, once again, on blind passion or unquestioning tradition, the functions now served by libraries will continue to remain at the heart of our society, and so long as this is true we shall need men and women of superior ability and superior training to see that these services are well performed.

2. COMPARATIVE STUDY OF LIBRARY SYSTEMS

CARL M. WHITE

"BASES" as used in the general title may refer either to separate geographical locations or to the fundamental principles of a subject. The two meanings correspond to two purposes of the present work. One is to introduce beginning students to librarianship as practised in selected countries whose work has attracted the attention of librarians elsewhere. The second is to illuminate problems of theory by examining librarianship in different social settings.

The problems involved in adapting libraries to the needs of readers are similar the world over. Different people solve them differently, but sooner or later the library procedures of a country begin to settle into a pattern. Accordingly the three resident lecturers, from Britain, Germany and the United States, were asked to describe characteristic procedures in their countries—methods of governing, organizing and financing libraries; methods of cataloging and classification; methods of giving good service to readers, etc. But of course modern librarianship is a more complex phenemenon than local-library methodology, important as that is. Therefore, each lecturer was also asked to describe his country's library program considered as a whole. "Program" as used here suggests the presence of system, of orderly planning, the over-all library policy that a nation is following. The task accordingly was one of articulating the goals and standards consciously or unconsciously used by the architects of the system as well as one of assessing national accomplishments in terms of these goals and standards.

Using these specifications, the following chapters tell what librarianship is like country by country, and this is all that can be expected of papers prepared independently of one another. Comparative librarianship is a subject which deals with material on theory and practice found in different geographical and political areas, but it is a method of study as well as a subject. The purpose of this chapter is to use this method to identify some of the common characteristics, or tendencies, which emerge from empirical study of the three nations named above. Where brief listing of common characteristics is sufficient, especially in the light of later chapters, little discussion is added. Other common features can be found besides those mentioned. The object is not so much to exhaust the subject as to illustrate the use of the comparative method and thus suggest the fruitfulness of applying it in further study of library problems. These problems, instead of remaining, as once they were, the province of a few nations, are taking on global proportions. At any rate, here are common characteristics worth noting:

I. TREND AWAY FROM PERSONAL LIBRARIES AND IMITATIONS OF THEM

The story of man's early reliance on libraries which the individual owned and administered as he saw fit, need not be further elaborated except to stress the fact that as learning expanded, privately operated libraries became too costly to keep up to date. German universities developed the seminar library as an aid to academic work and it helped bridge the transition to dependence on public-supported libraries for professional purposes. The innovation gained popularity in the nineteenth century when America and other younger nations were relying heavily on these pioneering universities for advanced training in scholarship. Returning students planted libraries of a similar nature in their own countries, and they took deep root.

The seminar library resembles, in convenience, organization, use of space and how it is controlled, a personal library, and some scholars remain strongly attached to it for precisely this reason. It is the model they are accustomed to and like. But while the seminar library, along with libraries which are organized and administered along similar lines, still survives and flourishes, no major country accepts it any longer as the best model to use when planning further library advances. There are several reasons why it is being superseded, but they add up to saying that it is giving ground to the same forces which pushed aside the once all-sufficient personal library. Since the nineteenth century, intellectual materials have continued to increase at a prodigious rate. There are more fields, with more overlapping interests, as well as more publications in each one. In all important fields, there are also more scholars and students. And on top of all this, the practice of drawing heavily on the literature, which the seminar library was created to foster has become so commonplace that it is now standard practice throughout this vastly enlarged community of learned people. The seminar library is designed best to serve the private interests of a small group, whereas we now live in a day when library service must, in fairness to all scholars and all taxpayers, be planned to serve the greatest good of the greatest number at minimum cost. When the popularity of the seminar library was at its crest, one American university, the University of Chicago, projected a library system which would give each department its own library. The very thoroughness and fairness with which the system was planned helped to make it vividly apparent how poorly adapted it is to the needs of a new day in scholarship, and how expensive it would be to maintain a system which ate up so much space, demanded such expensive duplication of books and personnel, and made such inefficient use of suitable hours of opening. This demonstrated inability to serve justly, efficiently and economically the twentieth century's greatly enlarged community of serious readers has forced a search for some design or model better adapted to the needs of the times. This brings us to the next point.

2. INSTITUTION OF LIBRARY SERVICE AS A PUBLIC RESPONSIBILITY

Provision of library service at public expense is now the established policy of the three nations whose experience is being drawn on most in this review. The total financial cost each year amounts to sums hardly dreamed of in the nineteenth century.

The procedure for carrying out this policy is by no means uniform, but the prevailing tendency is: to recognize library service as a new social responsibility to be delegated, in the same way as other work requiring high personal and academic qualifications, to professionally trained personnel; to place the work on an economic footing, to enable those who make it a full-time career to live in dignity and self-respect; and to create a hierarchy of positions in the field by which the most able rise to top positions of leadership. In sociological terms, modern society has reached the stage where a new division of specialized labor concerned with books and people has arisen, and responsibility for this new work is being institutionalized, with all that this means in organization, recruiting and training of personnel, professional status, and responsibility for social leadership.

As already intimated, however, there are being built up at public expense many collections for which the library profession has no responsibility whatsoever. The best examples are in universities, where a professor may exercise a degree of personal control over university-owned books which differs little, if at all, from the sort of control he would exercise if they belonged to him. Of course a scholar must have books. Furthermore, special subsidies are required to get certain types of work done. The combination of these two things has produced confusion, even heated debate, as to whether the purpose of public support of book purchase for universities is to subsidize the work of the individual scholar or to help finance a public service which may benefit him but which he is not empowered to control to the disadvantage of others.

Each nation must decide for itself which activities it will subsidize and which it will institutionalize. Meanwhile those communities, where library systems of the highest quality are developing appear to be those which institute library service as a bona fide public responsibility. By this term is meant acceptance by the state, or by some philanthropic body, of responsibility not only for financing, but at the same time for regulating and controlling the service independent of the individuals thus served. An analogous process is the organization of a public school system to relieve families of some of the responsibility of educating their children—or the organization of a hospital to aid in caring for the sick. The private citizen benefits from the new service, but good citizenship calls on him in return to comply cheerfully with regulations designed to serve the common good. If any regulation is found detrimental to the common good, democratic government provides orderly ways of making changes.

3. LIBRARIES OF FOUR MAJOR TYPES

Certain countries have national libraries. The Library of Congress and the British Museum Library function as such in a general way, but Britain, Germany and the United States are alike in having no national library in any formal sense of the term.

They are alike also in having well-developed systems of libraries comprising four major types. The terminology used to describe them varies, even in one country, while the extent to which librarians treat these several types as branches of a single profession (or instead as a cluster of special fields which have little in common except the name "library") differs from country to country even more. Terminology aside, the literature shows substantial agreement on what might called the social basis of the four types. One type has risen to serve the needs of higher learning and research and is often referred to as the academic and research library. Academic instruction and research are of course not the same thing, but the clienteles of those libraries which fall in this general category overlap so much that separating them into two classes is considered artificial.

A second type provides library service for students in lower schools. It originated, as did the academic and research library, as a result of literate society's growing dependence on letters as the main source of contact with accumulated thought, but it exists to serve a younger clientele. School librarianship came late. As an organized movement, it can hardly be said to go back further than World War I and most librarians would put the date later than that.

Once members of the younger generation are equipped through lower and higher schools for adult life, they enter their chosen callings and there they find people across the whole spectrum of practical affairs (in government, the professions, business and industry) making constant and necessary use of information and information sources in their daily work. These demands for information to be applied to the business of everyday living began to be felt in the nineteenth century, and an organized movement to create appropriate information services got under way early in the twentieth. It gave birth to organizations variously referred to as special libraries, information bureaux, and documentation centres. Librarians less sensitive to the undercurrents forcing these services into being greeted efforts to organize them with inertia and even opposition. It was unfortunate, for the new movement became in part as a result a protest movement, introducing confusion and disunity where mutual understanding and harmony would have been, and still is, more fitting. This stress on the importance of the third type of library links up with the treatment in the last chapter of the ways that a civilized man's deepening dependence on accumulating intelligence found expression in institutional form. Seen in this perspective, modern information services are part of an institution which could go by any name but which for lack of a better is called the modern library movement. Indeed these services mark a sort of culmination of this movement—the step where the use of letters or organized intelligence or information leaves the cloister to be taken out into the office, workshop, market-place.

The special library thus resembles the keystone in the arch which some builders at first rejected. Its peculiarities grow out of deliberate effort and skill exerted to satisfy the information requirements of a specific clientele, often limited to members of some organization or other. As a rule, this type of library concentrates less on procedures which are common in libraries of other types and specializes on getting published or unpublished information for specific, carefully anticipated uses. It also goes beyond the normal standard of library service in getting the information in the shape to be put to work at once with a minimum effort on the part of a clientele which may not consider themselves "readers" in the accepted sense at all.

The fourth class, the public library, stands at the other extreme as a sort of beacon for the community as a whole. Sometimes it is overshadowed by the academic and research library and may venture but casually if at all into information services or into serving readers of school or pre-school age. When its usefulness is thus circumscribed, it is fittingly called the "popular library", meaning a library which specializes in providing leisure reading and entertainment. As is recognized, however, the public library at its best is a more virile force than that. Public librarians make a point of cooperating with and helping out library services available elsewhere in the community, and this fact at first has a negative suggestion about its role; but is another way of describing a range of interest, a flexibility which enable it to respond to the demands of scholars or school children or businessmen whenever the good of the community requires it. One of the later chapters (chap. 4) speaks of the foundations of the public library. The treatment there and elsewhere suggests that, in those countries where literacy and literate habits are deepening and where the academic and research library has not branched out to bear the responsibility, the public library has been in process of becoming the broad base or foundation of the entire national library system. Its clientele consists of common people who, with the progress of enlightened ways, are developing an uncommon number of specialities, many of which require the use of intellectual resources of one kind or another.

4. SIMILAR NATIONAL LIBRARY OBJECTIVES

Libraries provide services which are so numerous that it would take several pages to detail them. While they vary a great deal from one library to another, they have a certain family resemblance the world over, so it is not surprising to find attempts made to classify them. A sample classification is to be found in *Library Trends* volume 3, page 148–163 where it is suggested that most of the hundreds of services available in libraries of various types can be grouped under the following headings: free lending of library materials for use, personal assistance by a trained staff in helping the reader get what he wants, counseling and teaching which go beyond ordinary reference service, preparation and publication of library tools, information services which save the inquirer the trouble of doing the necessary research for himself, building library collections, and other technical services which take place behind the scenes but which are important in procuring, conserving and organizing library materials for present or future use.

Notwithstanding the fact that the use of letters and learning, and therefore of libraries, has slowly been built into the structure of literate society, any attempt to isolate library services to society from services to individual readers runs into the same kind of difficulty that troubled Browning's Fra Lippo Lippi who, enjoined to paint spirit, found himself everlastingly painting the flesh. Comparative study of library systems reveals that the social functions they perform do in fact differ from one another. The difference is radical, for example, between West Germany and Germany under the Nazis. The library programs of the countries on which this survey is based are much alike. Essentially, their library objectives are as follows:

To accumulate and make available now and in the future the best work of the mind, regardless of when or where the work was done. This is the task of conserving those intellectual resources which may be said to document in any significant respect the experience of the race. Man stands to benefit in very practical ways from having at hand the best of his cultural heritage, but some obligation is felt to retain it not merely for practical benefit but for its own sake. Opinion varies, however, on just what material should be conserved strictly for its own sake.

To afford access to all responsible intellectual work without interference from political or religious authority. These countries adhere to a policy of making the results of serious intellectual work freely accessible. The following statement made by a public official of high rank in one country expresses a tolerance found in all three of them. "If this nation is to be wise as well as strong, if we are to achieve our destiny, then we need more new ideas for more wise men reading more good books in more public libraries. These libraries should be open to all—except the censor. We must know all the facts and hear all the alternatives and listen to all the criticisms. Let us welcome controversial authors."

To further research. Some subjects can be studied with little or no reference to the literature, but nearly all important research nowadays depends on knowing what has been done, and is being done, by other workers. It is impossible to keep abreast of the status of knowledge in rapidly advancing fields without having at hand a well-equipped library of sources for reference. Provision of suitable materials and services is costly, but usually cheaper than trying to get along without knowing what else has been done.

To aid formal instruction. Textbooks and lectures have their place, but all three countries rely less on these in most subjects than formerly and rely proportionately more on the use of the library as an aid to instruction. A good many progressive thinkers have come to treat the library as the heart of instruction; more is said on this subject in later chapters. The central role it now plays comes about as a result of three influences. First is the greatly increased and rapidly increasing number of well-written books which will facilitate and broaden the student's comprehension of the subject. Second is a gradual reform in methods of instruction, brought about by research on the learning process. The evidence establishes that learning is more effective when the learner's work is so planned as to stimulate him to master the subject he studies through at least some independent work in a library instead of depending on lectures alone or combining them with required readings. Third, re-examination of the purposes of formal education has led many to conclude that one objective should be to encourage people while they are still young to form a life-time habit of reading. Habits of course are formed only through exercise. It follows that students at all levels of instruction should first of all have access to libraries which are well-stocked with good books to read. They should moreover have a chance to live in an atmosphere, complete with good library service, which stimulates the forming of this habit. An inescapable obligation thus falls on teachers and librarians to work together to help young people learn for themselves the enjoyment of reading and this includes the supplying of sympathetic guidance which young people require in these matters. Experience has shown that required readings can create distaste for reading, rather than pleasure, but this outcome is unusual. Meanwhile it is widely agreed that a student may graduate from some universities without learning how to work independently, perhaps even without ever knowing the tingle of excitement which good reading can bring; but it is also agreed that no such graduate can be called literate or cultivated in the higher meaning of the term.

To supply information in the management of practical affairs. For a long time, the advancement of knowledge was an enterprise which was considered separate, indeed aloof, from the business of the man in the street. Literate society, it has been observed, is quite as much a process as a static condition—a process of permeating all phases of life with the practice of obtaining and using the best available information in deciding and doing things of all kinds. The very success of the advancement of knowledge in the erudite sense of the term taught the man in the street how to improve on the older techniques which relied on tradition or on snap judgment wherever tradition failed to show the way. It has also been observed that the rise of a branch of library activity specially concerned with procuring reliable information and putting it to work marks the breakdown of the older idea that knowledge belongs in the cloister apart from the bustling world outside. A literate society makes use of the scientific process and the results of careful inquiry in any and every sphere of human effort.

To promote popular enlightenment and to enrich human life. Every free man has an inalienable right to remain as ignorant as he pleases once he meets compulsory school-attendance requirements; but the attitude of these three nations, and others, is that when any citizen chooses to exercise this right others suffer. For self-government is an empty, retreating ideal unless citizens resolutely qualify themselves to decide intelligently the various issues which determine how the people are to be governed. The level of popular enlightenment thus becomes a barometer of self-government to which a people can rise: it is a sobering fact that in general we get the quality of government which we first qualify ourselves to demand.

The free library has come to be prized as a special aid to popular enlightenment, but its role in deciding issues of state is incidental to a more basic purpose of democracy which is often overlooked. It is a sacred tenet of free men's faith that nobody is to be considered merely as a tool of the state. It is rather the other way around. The state is a tool to aid in the highest cultural and spiritual development of all the people. Libraries are prized for many services, but self-governing communities prize them for nothing more than in helping each person rise to and live at the full height of his powers. By putting such things first, the population better enables itself as a matter of course to handle its political affairs.

5. SPECIALIZED LITERATURE ON THE ART AND SCIENCE OF LIBRARIANSHIP

The characteristics of the literature in these three countries are not the same, but in general the birth of an organized profession has been accompanied by publication of journals to use in exchanging ideas, and by production of library tools including labor-saving manuals, guides to good library practice, and aids of all kinds for the use of readers. The sharing of experience and improving of tools to work with are tasks that are never finished: the publishing activities of major library organizations give these things high priority now as they did to start with. Critics of the literature, if they complain that too much writing is didactic and shallow, wisely refrain from objecting to these purposes.

The gradual acceptance of library science as a university responsibility has been accompanied on one side by rising standards for the education of librarians and on the other by more competent critical analysis of library problems. If a particular date is singled out to mark the beginning of an attendant change in the literature, perhaps the most appropriate one would be the launching of the *Library Quarterly* by the Graduate Library School of the University of Chicago in 1931. During the interval numerous monographs reporting results of careful scholarship have taken their place on library science shelves alongside work reported by the *Quarterly*, but the change is more pervasive than outstanding individual contributions by Joeckel, Wilson, Tauber, Bryan, Shaw, Shera, or others. Better educated librarians are doing more substantial work, and this is subtly influencing the literature.

To these three branches of literature, others can be added. The "survey" has been perfected as an administrative tool of the first importance. It is sometimes described as an application of the methods of objective research to a particular library situation. This is good as far as it goes, but the survey does not stop with reporting the results of research. In the technical sense in which it has come to be employed the term survey also involves the application of expert judgment in proposing what should be done about the situation. This clearly is something that goes beyond research as ordinarily understood. Second, considerable source material is being produced by systematically gathering and publishing data on various subjects ranging from library salaries to the rate at which book collections are growing and how much they cost. Third are systematic treatises on school libraries, university libraries, technical libraries, or other aspects of librarianship such as reference work and "technical services". General texts of this kind are not yet available in all fields. For example, a comprehensive treatise on the modern public library, for the use of the beginning student, is not to be found. Fourth, there is a voluminous amount of library legislation, badly scattered. Even a cursory account should not omit the vast amount of writing, referred to as "promotional", which interprets the meaning of librarianship. Much of this writing has no permanent value, but here the librarian customarily makes his bid for public understanding of his mission.

6. BIBLIOGRAPHICAL ACCESS TO LIBRARY HOLDINGS

Access to books and related materials may be provided by removing all barriers and permitting readers to go directly to the shelves. This is called physical access, or more often "open access". The latter phrase was coined when the idea was new and librarians were experimenting with methods by which they could successfully break away from the practice of keeping books behind closed doors or behind other barriers to ready access. Although open access is spreading with the growth of influence of the public library, the practice is by no means universal.

Bibliographical access refers to any method of gaining access to books through bibliographies, published or unpublished. Thus when the reader goes to a library and finds a printed catalog or a card catalog where all of its holdings are listed, we say he has bibliographical access to the holdings of the library.

All three countries have invested thousands of hours of time in listing the contents of their libraries. Long experience has shown that the material needed by a reader can most conveniently be located if he is able to approach it either by author, subject or title (if the title is a distinctive one). In general, the libraries of these countries have each a carefully prepared catalog which provides all three approaches. The service does not stop there. Normally a reader may in a few days' time ascertain whether a book he cannot obtain through his own library can be obtained from some other library; for libraries in each country cooperate to obtain material wherever it is located, and books may also be borrowed from other countries.

The three plans to facilitate bibliographical access thus have similar objectives and, up to a point, use similar methods. Examples of similarities include: spread in the practice of depending on card catalogs instead of printed catalogs, the use of author and title entries, and the listing of all the holdings of a library and its branches in a central catalog. The most pronounced difference is in subject approach. The issue is whether to have a classified catalog or an alphabetical (dictionary) catalog with cross references.

It is a complex problem. Arguments for the classified catalog start from the value of thorough systematization of knowledge. This method brings all related material together and, moreover, shows what the relationship is. The inquirer in locating a particular work thus finds beside it works on the same subject and works on all cognate branches as well. It is a service of such usefulness in much academic work that studies have shown scholars of different nations to prefer good classified catalogs. The problem of locating specific subjects in the classification scheme is usually facilitated by the availability of a separate alphabetical list of subjects.

The dictionary catalog arose during the early days of the modern library movement as part of a revolutionary movement to make of books, libraries and reading a force more significant than they were at the time. The pioneers of the movement agreed on a general strategy aimed at bringing more readers and more good books together. It was a many-sided effort which involved developing better librarians, more attractive libraries and methods of attracting readers to the libraries; but it also involved breaking down the then-existing barriers to books. One decision made was that readers would be served best if the books were arranged on the shelves in classified order and if ways could be found to open the shelves so readers could go directly to the books. Open access, it was argued, is better than any kind of intermediary—whether a classified catalog, a dictionary catalog, a reference librarian or reader's adviser.

The classified catalog was widely in use then and was, as now, in great favor among the more sophisticated readers especially those who were familiar with the scheme in use. However, the reader who was not familiar with the library found it a barrier and it took time to educate him on how to use it. The dictionary catalog was found to be easier to learn.

Theories of subject cataloging thus impinge on other questions. One is whether bibliographical access is to be used as a supplement to direct access to the books on the shelves or as the only means of access. A related question is whether the primary purpose of the library catalog is to be a tool for locating some work in a particular library or whether it is a more ambitious bibliographical tool designed to show the organization of the universe of knowledge. There is no disagreement as to the importance, especially for scholars, of classified bibliography. There is however no agreement that the best, most economical way to render this service is to construct independent catalogs based on the holdings of individual

c

libraries. The difference in approach is thus seen to go beyond the respective merits of the classified catalog and the dictionary catalog. The two forms are each part of a larger strategy which an energetic, library-minded nation has worked out for the service of its people; so they must be evaluated in terms of what they contribute to the success of the total system within which they are constructed. Meanwhile the objectives of both systems are similar and if members of the international fraternity of librarians find improvements they can make by borrowing from their neighbors, these adaptations we may be sure will be made as soon as they can be fitted into the system they work with.

7. ACTIVE PROFESSIONAL ORGANIZATIONS

A library movement is made of people. Till far into the nineteenth century, this was not realized; librarianship was considered more a matter of physical things which a clerk could care for—books, rooms, tables, etc. The library movement in each of these countries has been furthered, especially at the beginning, by scholars and public-spirited citizens who recognized the worth of libraries and who aided in creating full-time positions of rank where the gifts of capable librarians could find full scope. Higher education for librarians was inaugurated in America and Germany in the early 1880's, and from this point leadership began to pass over to specially trained full-time workers. But earlier, in 1876, the American Library Association was founded and the next year, in Britain, the Library Association. No date can be set for the beginning of the modern library movement, but the spiral of achievements associated with it begins in the fourth quarter of the nineteenth century which followed these first steps. Professional organizations have served as effective forums for the discussion of national library problems. They have given librarians a channel for making themselves heard; and through contacts with other organizations, government agencies and the general public have greatly influenced public sentiment and action on libraries. They have been particularly helpful in developing and promoting adoption of national standards affecting personnel as well as major aspects of library organizations and service.

8. DEVELOPMENT OF HUMAN RESOURCES

If one digs into the organization of libraries in these countries, few things stand out more plainly than the hardly surprising fact that librarians of stature are not found in little libraries. It is not that the smallest library cannot benefit from the finest talents: it is a matter of applying the idea that an individual library program, the same as the library movement as a whole, is made more of people than of things. The administration of libraries still shows traces of an older idea when the human element was not wisely utilized. The neglect is apparent in perpetuating seminar and small departmental libraries in poorly coordinated university library systems, in the number of weak public libraries which operate independently of libraries elsewhere in the same region, in indifference to separating clerical and professional responsibilities so as to make better use of different levels of ability in the same library. It is instructive to observe by way of contrast how uniformly international experience shows that good library service to a community cannot be given without an annual expenditure of several thousand marks, pounds or dollars. There is of course no magic in fixed sums of money, for the thing at stake is not of a material nature. It is rather a tangible manifestation of the fact that an effective program of service entails, over and above everything else, a program of effort involving a sizable pyramid of human energies. At the base are jobs for manual workers and clerks while at the top are jobs capable of attracting and holding professional talents of a high order. This explains the tendency to develop larger units of service in all these countries. A library too small to provide scope for a hierarchy of well-organized human talent kills the whole possibility of library service of high quality.

9. WELL-DESIGNED LIBRARY BUILDINGS

The history of library housing falls roughly into three periods: (1) when space was used that was not specially planned for library purposes; (2) the era of the monument to letters and learning when beauty and magnificence were stressed but criteria of excellence for library service were not well understood; and (3) the era since professional librarians and a new generation of architects began to learn how to work together. Their combined efforts have radically changed the whole planning process and produced a new conception of what a library building should be and do. The best buildings have been erected since World War II in the United States and Germany. By today's criteria, few buildings before that date would rate very high.

As soon as one stops to reflect, it is apparent that much of the difference between the attainable and the unattainable depends on space—on distance, geographical relationships. It is this simple insight that accounts mainly for the revolution in the planning of library buildings. As an example, one of the objectives of the modern library is to attract people to the library—not to wait for people to take the initiative themselves. Experience has shown that one of the ways to bring people and books together is to select a site close to where two main arteries of pedestrian traffic intersect, then plan an exterior as well as an interior which generously exhibits attractive books, thus arresting the attention of passersby. One college faculty decided at the suggestion of the librarian to do all it could with a new building to encourage students to read books related to the ones on the regular reading lists provided them by professors. The solution was to place shelving in the middle of the first floor where required readings in a subject—say history—could be surrounded by a generous selection of related works among which students would be free to browse at will. It is one of many imaginative departures from tradition that have been made in the newer library buildings which has proved very successful and is now being copied elsewhere. When the student leaves this building, he is forced by physical arrangements to pass close to an attendant who checks to see that all books are properly charged, but aside from this control, he is free to move at will among thousands of books and recordings, newspapers and magazines, all on open shelves with good lighting and comfortable chairs similar to those one might expect to find in other well-appointed "living" rooms.

These are but a few examples of the way space is being shaped by exceptionally careful planning to aid in the achievement of educational objectives. No staff member works more effectively than the well-planned building to maintain standards of library service of high quality. It has the added advantage of durability.

Conclusion. This survey is intended to serve three purposes. One purpose is to suggest the usefulness of comparative study, which has not been used as much as certain other methods to aid the advancement of librarianship. Second, library systems like freezing water tend to lose fluidity as their lines harden with time. Nations where library development is still plastic have a chance to benefit from the wealth of international experience that is now available. Mistakes themselves may be instructive, but the attempt has been made here to codify prevailing tendencies which have more positive application as possible guide lines or minimum specifications in the planning of a national library program. Third, the following chapters bring perhaps as much material together for this purpose as is to be found between any other pair of covers, and the final purpose is to assist in relating these contributions to one another.

3. BOOKS AND LIBRARIES IN OUR TIME I:
INTRODUCTION OF THE FIRST LECTURER

ORD. PROF. SUUT KEMAL YETKIN
Rector of the University of Ankara

IF one were to ask a person who was compelled to live on a desolate island what he would take with him there, he would not consider a razor and pyjamas as of first importance if he were a man, nor lipstick and evening dresses, if she were a woman. Granted a few of the most necessary essentials for living, such a person would undoubtedly put books first.

Man can renounce many things, but not books. Who would not take some books with him on a trip—provided of course he is not illiterate? It is true, we might be more absorbed by the scenery than the books during much of the journey, but we like to keep them with us just the same. Were all books to disappear suddenly, how unbearable life would be! We cannot think of the world without men, and we cannot think of intelligent men without books. For a literate person there is no place more comfortable, more deeply satisfying than his library.

Increasing developments in the fields of science and arts, and the impossibility of buying all the books needed, forced men to pass beyond the narrow bounds of their own personal libraries, and in the course of time state and university libraries were founded to meet increasing needs for books which individual people, unaided, could not meet.

There is not any civilized country today which does not have great libraries. History teaches us the invaluable riches of the libraries founded in Kuttuba by Spanish Ommiades, in Baghdad by Abbasides, and elsewhere as civilization advanced. During the nineteenth and especially the twentieth century, books have increased tremendously in number, and they are read more and more. One great library after another has been founded in all progressive countries.

The century we live in is a century of specialization. When new study and research fields appear, new professions and invariably new subdivisions within these professions develop. The lively movement of librarianship paved the way for a new field of specialization. This is the specialization of people who work side by side with scholars and accept library science and library development as their professional responsibility.

In Turkey we have distinguished libraries and librarians actively promoting the development of the country and the betterment of library science and library services. To achieve the highest degree of success in this field, we have to know what has been done and is being done in other countries. The International Series of Lectures in Librarianship, which we inaugurate here today, has been arranged with this purpose in mind.

The Faculty of Letters, with the help of some sister countries, will bring here librarians who excel in their profession to represent and explain the library experience of their countries to this select audience.

We are happy to see our first lecturer, Miss Lucile Morsch, among us today. She is Deputy Chief Assistant Librarian of the Library Congress. Before reaching this important post in one of the biggest libraries of the world, Miss Morsch graduated from Iowa State University and then obtained first the degree of Bachelor of Science in library science and then the degree of Master of Science at Columbia University. When she was still in her twenties, she edited a bibliography, one result of which was to show how rapidly the literature of the library field was increasing. This work was prepared so well and filled such an important gap that it became the starting point of an invaluable set that all major libraries have today. This success has not only helped prepare her for her present important post, but was followed with work which brought her fresh honour. For her great success in cataloging and classification, which is as important for American libraries as it is for Turkish libraries, she was given the Margaret Mann Award in 1951. More recently she was elected President of the American Library Association. This is the highest honour American librarians can give one of their colleagues.

The first lecture to be presented by Miss Morsch is the *Foundations of the American Public Library*. The second lecture, on *Academic and Research Libraries in the United States*, is to be given next Tuesday at the same hour in the same auditorium.

I invite her to give her first lecture.

4. FOUNDATIONS OF THE AMERICAN PUBLIC LIBRARY

LUCILE M. MORSCH

Library of Congress, Washington

I HAVE accepted the invitation to discuss the American public library with a Turkish audience with great humility. I am sure that nothing that has been accomplished by that institution will be recorded for posterity as a contribution to the world's culture comparable in even a minute degree to that of your ancient libraries. If all the American public libraries should suddenly be destroyed by a great holocaust, the loss to the world would probably be less than if a similar fate should befall your treasuries of unique manuscript books with their exquisite illuminations. No one can help but be deeply impressed by the remarkable renaissance that has taken place in Turkey in recent years and the progressiveness of your country which is shown by economic, political, and social developments as well as cultural advances. It is exciting, to me as a librarian, to know that your national library, under the distinguished direction of Dr. Ötüken, epitomizes this renaissance and this progressiveness. The ambitious program which he envisioned for this library and which he is so successfully carrying out, and the dynamic leadership that he has been giving to the Turkish library movement, make me realize that I am carrying coals to Newcastle. Nevertheless, it is probably safe to assume that you know as little about this work and its significance as a similar audience in the United States would know of the scope and services of the Library of Congress and of public libraries generally beyond local boundaries. On this assumption, and because libraries have played such an important role in the development of the United States, I accept every opportunity to make their story better known whether at home or abroad.

American librarians have such faith in education and the power of the printed word that as a class they can almost be said to believe that only books and reading are going to save the world. In consequence of my personal faith in the contribution that libraries can make to the better life I have used every chance I have had to persuade my own Government—through its operation of American libraries in other countries, its exchange of persons programs, and its technical assistance programs in countries less highly developed economically than the United States

—to put more emphasis on library programs. Likewise, as a member of the United States National Commission for UNESCO, I take every opportunity to point out the necessity of universal library development for the attainment of the objectives of the United Nations Educational, Scientific and Cultural Organization.

No other country could successfully transplant to its own shores the average public library of the United States, but every country can learn from our experience and can profit from our failures as well as from our successes. Having referred to the "average" public library of the United States, I must emphasize that there is no such thing as the "average" American public library. A little historical background is necessary to explain the diversity.

If the American librarian is inclined to believe that libraries can save the world it is without question because he is a creature of his environment. From our colonial days, the American people have put great stock in education. As the pioneers moved westward from the Atlantic coast, they settled around churches and schools. Preachers and teachers occupied positions of great respect. The parent's ambition to see that his children had a better education than he himself had had was a characteristic of the early settlers that has been handed down from generation to generation. Lack of roads and communication between the villages in our sparsely-settled land meant that local institutions developed to meet local needs and on the initiative of the villagers themselves.

Books were scarce and difficult to come by. They had been brought from England with the first settlers and were treasured for the special worth they had in a new country with an extraordinary thirst for knowledge. It is not surprising that our first libraries should have been established by the simple pooling of the books owned by small groups of men who formed societies for the purpose of sharing their books. More than sixty of these libraries were established before the colonies declared their independence in 1776. Strange as it may seem, these society libraries felt a civic responsibility from the time of their establishment and provided for membership on the part of any inhabitant of their towns. They considered themselves public libraries.

In the next period in our history subscription libraries flourished. These were similar to the society libraries except that they required only an annual membership fee, which made them available to many more people. They made such a firm place for themselves that some of them still exist as private membership libraries; for example, the Boston Athenaeum and the New York Society Library.

These forerunners of the free public library in the United States explain many of the characteristics of today's libraries. Foremost among these is their individualism and the emphasis they place on tailoring their services to local needs. The American public librarian today makes community surveys to learn as much as he can about his community. He then selects his books in accordance with the educational level, the occupations, interests, activities, and needs of the population. He also considers the availability of books from bookstores and other local sources. He initiates library services to supplement the services of other institutions (schools, colleges, churches, theaters, art galleries, clubs, etc.) in the community, and not to duplicate them. For example, if each school has its own library, he expects the school library to fill all needs related to school assignments, and he can concentrate on leisure time reading and books on extra-curricular subjects, so far as patrons of school age are concerned. If the local schools do not yet have their own libraries, the public library may lend classroom collections to the school to enrich its teaching. Many churches in our cities have circulating libraries for their members. The nature and size of these may affect the demands made on the public library for certain types of books.

The small group of proprietors of the society or subscription library has been succeeded by a board of trustees, in most of our libraries. These are laymen (doctors, lawyers, bankers, business men) who give their services as public-spirited citizens to establishing the policies of their library. They select the librarian and advise him or her on the conduct of the library. They are responsible for the operation of the library but in most cases they delegate the management to a professional librarian who is appointed for an indefinite period. Thus the public library is primarily a local institution which is entirely dependent upon local enthusiasm and interest for its maintenance and development. It has always been a source of local pride, even when it was a miserable, poorly-supported library providing minimum services. The reason for this is that practically all of our public libraries, great and small, were started with the vision and enthusiasm of a single individual as its chief assets. We still have many small, struggling village libraries which are not supported by taxes and must depend upon funds raised by interested citizens through card parties, sales of home-baked goods, amateur entertainments, etc. These libraries are open only a few hours a week and are manned by volunteer workers or ill-paid ladies with leisure time but no professional training. Such libraries are fast disappearing, however, because of state and federal assistance to libraries in rural areas and in small villages and towns, and because of a trend in the United States toward the development of library systems. In a library system the inadequate small library may join with neighboring small libraries to enjoy some of the advantages of a larger library. I shall have more to say later about state and federal assistance and library systems.

As a distinctly local institution, the public library strives to be a community center that will attract as large a part of the townspeople as possible. There is ample evidence that if people can only be exposed to books they will catch the desire to read just as they will "catch" smallpox if they are exposed to the smallpox germ. The librarian's first task then is to bring books and people together. This is the justification for the library to provide a small auditorium or a meeting room in the library for any club or organization in the town that may wish to use it. The garden club, for example, may start holding its monthly meeting in the library simply because it has too many members to continue meeting in their homes. The librarian will take advantage of such a specialized audience to display appropriate books and may prepare a special reading list of books and periodical articles to enrich the programs of the meetings. The club may originate with the limited purpose of providing its members with the opportunity to discuss gardening experiences and perhaps to exchange small plants and cuttings with each other. The contribution made by the library may mean that the discussions are soon extended both in depth and breadth. The club members' interests will range from flower arrangement to more, and more beautiful, city parks. In return for the assistance of the librarian, who will continue to bring appropriate new books to the attention of the club, its members may take the responsibility for keeping the library supplied with an arrangement of cut flowers to make its entrance hall more inviting, it may advise the librarian on the selection of books in its fields of interest, or it may even contribute financially to their purchase.

Bringing books and people together may also result from the library's sponsorship of lectures, discussion groups, film showings, concerts, and exhibits of various kinds in the library. The library also goes outside its walls to distribute booklists and information about the library. The librarian and other members of his professional staff participate actively in as many community activities as they can; they use the mass media— newspapers, radio, and television—to make the library's services known.

The most important advertisement for a library's services, however, is the basic service itself that a professionally-trained library staff can give with a good collection of books, periodicals, newspapers, phonograph records, maps, and even—in many libraries—motion pictures and paintings, housed in comfortable quarters. In this listing of librarian, the collection, and the library building, I put the librarian first because it is his knowledge and skill that is needed to make a collection of books into a library, his selection and acquisition of the materials that will meet the needs of his community, his organization of the collection for use, and his success in bringing books and people together. Although the library building is unquestionably the least important of the three, it is an essential ingredient in developing library services and attracting many of the people who can benefit from them. Hence, great emphasis is placed on locating the library in the most convenient and accessible spot, on making it as attractive as a department store, as easy to use as a supermarket, as bright and cheerful and comfortable as a private living room.

The services are tailored to fit both individuals and groups. The public library has always emphasized its work with individuals and has taken pride in the many success stories that showed the influence of the library on a person's achievements. Some librarians have specialized as readers' advisers to assist individuals in a planned program of reading that will fulfil their needs and desires. This is one of the ways in which the public library has earned its description as the university of the people.

Work with groups may refer to services to different age groups in the library, and to the work with clubs, and churches, and schools outside the library. Special services to children, for example, were among the first to be developed. Realizing that a lifetime reading habit is a priceless possession, librarians have tried to attract patrons at a tender age. With separate rooms for the children, where the furnishings and decor as well as the books are chosen to attract the youngest readers and even children of the picture-book age who have not yet learned to read, specially-trained librarians with a thorough knowledge of children's literature and a way with children have a golden opportunity to develop lifelong readers and lifelong library patrons. The work of our children's librarians with parents and writers and publishers may be almost as important as their work with children. The quality of children's books published in the United States in the last 35–40 years has improved tremendously, and without doubt children's librarians deserve much of the credit.

Services to adolescents and young adults, as we have come to call our youth in their upper teens, developed at a later date. Now, however, most of our larger libraries have special collections and specially-trained librarians to help this age group retain its interest in reading as it graduates from the children's department and may require guidance into the adult services.

The newest services to a clientele defined according to age has come from recognition of the needs of the aging. An increasing proportion of our population is moving into the category of "senior citizens"—men and women over the age of 65, most of them retired and unfamiliar with abundant leisure time. The public library has found that it can make a particular contribution to enriching the lives of this group, not only by providing books of special interest and books that will supply information they need in order to solve their new problems, but by creating entirely new interests for them through clubs or discussion groups that meet in the library.

Providing books of special interest, whether for recreation, for culture, or for information, is not limited to groups defined by age. Most of the larger public libraries are organized on a subject basis, with librarians who are also specialists in the literature of a particular subject field. For example, many libraries have a business department, where the books on economics and other subjects of particular interest to a business man, are shelved and serviced. A separate business branch of the public library, located in the heart of the business district of the city, is not unusual. A music department, with facilities to permit private listening to recorded music and a music librarian, is to be expected in the larger libraries.

Too many people think of the public library only as a source of re-creation and culture; too few realize its utilitarian objective of providing information. Nevertheless, the library has this objective in developing its book collection and in providing reference services. The professional man who is preparing a speech for the Rotary Club, the bride who needs information on home decoration, the traveller or the arm-chair traveller who wants to dispel his ignorance of another country and its people, the young man who wants to qualify for a new job by acquiring certain skills that he can teach himself—each of these calls upon the public library. There he will find most of the books of interest to him on open shelves, arranged by subject, usually according to the Dewey Decimal Classification. He will find the books listed in a card catalog according to their authors, according to their titles, and according to their subject content. He will find commercially-published indexes to the most-frequently consulted periodicals, that supplement the book collection and are often indispensable to provide desired information. He will be encouraged to browse among the books and choose those that interest him. He will also find a professional librarian eager to advise him on the best books for his needs and ready to assist him in the use of catalogs and indexes which serve as keys to the library's collection. If maps, pictures, filmstrips, phonograph records, or other forms of material in the library will help him, the librarian will direct him to such materials.

One highly-developed service of the public library is that of providing answers to specific inquiries. It is standard practice to go to the public library, or to obtain the information by telephone, for the myriads of facts that the patrons of a library need every day. Some of these may be amusing to the reference librarian, as for example, when a secretary, who does not want to admit to her "boss" that a word in a letter he has just dictated to her is beyond her vocabulary, calls the library to learn how to spell it; she can't find it in her own dictionary because she has only an abridged edition or because she can't spell the word. Some reference inquiries are made in emergencies, such as when the caller needs to know the antidote for a poison, what to do immediately when junior spills his chocolate milk on the new grey carpet, or facts for a newspaper story needed a half hour before press time. The reference librarian has at hand a more or less extensive collection, depending upon the size of the library, of dictionaries, encyclopedias, directories, and other so-called reference books that will provide factual information without delay.

All but the smallest public libraries go to the people, through branches or stations or by bookmobile. Some libraries give personal service to patients in hospitals and even to other shut-ins in their homes. Each subordinate library is a part of the library system. The books are all purchased, cataloged, and prepared for circulation in the main or central library. There are approximately 8000 public library systems in the United States, but almost 17,000 stationary service outlets and approximately 900 bookmobiles that serve the people who do not have a library accessible to them.

Public libraries are not all municipal libraries. Our fifty states are subdivided into some 3000 counties, and approximately a quarter of these have county libraries that serve the whole county directly; or they have a headquarters establishment in the county seat with branches and stations in villages, schools or crossroads centers, or with bookmobile service to such places. In addition, each state has one or more libraries at the state level to serve the state government and to provide some kinds of state-wide public library service. Generally there is a state library which lends boxes of books to schools and small libraries, and answers reference inquiries passed on from the librarians of the state when their own library resources are inadequate to answer the questions of their patrons. Most state libraries also give service directly to those inhabitants of the state who do not have access to a library; this service includes lending books by mail and replying to reference inquiries.

Then, the greatest public library in the nation towers over all the state, county, and municipal libraries—the Library of Congress. Although the Library of Congress is not generally thought of as a public library, because of its special responsibilities to the Congress of the United States and the Federal Government in Washington, it is open to the public, and those who use it receive services typical of those provided by any large public library, except that books are not generally lent for home reading. Only the members of Congress and their staffs, the highest officials of the Federal Government, and diplomatic representatives of other governments in Washington have this privilege. All other services are available to everyone who seeks them, with the exception of children. The Library of Congress does not provide library services to children; it does however, contain a substantial collection of children's books for the use of teachers, publishers, and other adults interested in children's literature. Although the bulk of the collections is housed in closed stacks, containing more than 250 miles of book shelves, from which they are brought to the reader at his specific request, more than 50,000 volumes and approximately 1300 current periodicals and newspapers are available on open shelves. These include, but are not limited to, encyclopedias, dictionaries, directories of all kinds, indexes and bibliographical publications. Professional reference librarians and subject specialists are available to assist the readers.

The Library of Congress receives more than 100,000 reference inquiries a year through correspondence. If the inquiry is one that probably could have been answered by the correspondent's local library a form letter suggesting that source for the information is sent in reply. If, however, the local resources have been exhausted, or the question is one that the Library of Congress is uniquely qualified to answer, a careful reply is prepared, regardless of whether the inquiry was received from a scholar of renown or from a school child.

Many of the Library's treasures are displayed from time to time in special exhibits; some of these are prepared as travelling exhibits and may be booked for showing in other cities over a period of two or three years. Some are even lent for showing in other countries, usually under the auspices of the United States Information Agency. The halls of the Library, partly because of these exhibits and partly because of the beauty of the main building—an ornate building in Italian Renaissance style which was completed in 1897—are a popular stop for tourists in the Nation's capital. Across the street from this building is the Library of Congress Annex, opened in 1939, and connected to the main building by a tunnel. The two buildings provide accommodations for readers in 21 general and special reading rooms. A third building is in the planning stage; it is urgently needed because the Library now contains nearly 39 million pieces including approximately 12 million volumes and pamphlets, of which roughly one third have been acquired since World War II.

Throughout the fall, winter, and spring seasons the Library presents numerous chamber music concerts, lectures, and poetry readings in a small auditorium in the main library building. These are made possible, free to the public, because of the generosity of several patrons of music and literature who have endowed the Library of Congress for this purpose.

Another service available to the general public, although fortunately only a small segment of the people requires this service, is the program of providing reading materials for the blind. This is a truly nation-wide service, because the Library and 30 other libraries serve various regions of the United States by lending books to blind readers. The annual appropriations made by the Congress of the United States to the Library of Congress include a substantial sum to make this possible. The Library of Congress is responsible for administering the program; this means that the Library is responsible for research and development to improve the program, for selecting the titles to be made available, and for having them manufactured, cataloged, and distributed to the regional libraries. Reading materials consist of books in raised characters, in Braille or Moon type, and books recorded on long-playing phonograph records, known as "talking books". The latter, of course, require that each reader be supplied with a machine on which the records can be played. The manufacture, distribution to state agencies (which in turn lend them to the blind readers) and repair of these machines are also the responsibility of the national library.

Without question, no account of public libraries in the United States can ignore the Library of Congress. I have mentioned, however, only very few of its services. More important still are the many bibliographic services, especially the sale of copies of its printed catalog cards, to other public libraries. Time will not permit me to elaborate on these services of a national library that are provided by the Library of Congress.

This sketch of the organization and services of the American public library shows you what a complex institution it is and suggests the qualifications required for the personnel in charge. I have indicated that it is a focal point in the community, that it must compete with other tax-supported services for its support, that it is a cultural, a recreational, and an educational institution tailored to the specific needs of the community. I have indicated that this means that its books are selected with the needs of the people—all the people—in mind, that the books are arranged in the library according to their subject matter, that librarians are available who know what is in the books and can advise the public on the best books for their needs, and who can themselves use the collection intensively to answer specific reference questions. I have suggested that the librarian must be a scholar who knows books and people; he must be an educator; he must be a business man or woman who can be responsible for spending public monies wisely; he must be an efficient administrator whether he runs a small library, which has no other professional librarian than he, or whether he runs the Library of Congress with its 2700 employees; he must have technical skills related to the acquisition of books and other library materials, technical skills to organize them for use through cataloging and classification, to bind and preserve books, and to bring books and readers together. You must be wondering whether there really are any such people, and I want to assure you that there are: men and women who have learned the art and science of librarianship through academic study and through the school of experience.

They have not worked alone. In 1876, they founded the American Library Association in order to share their knowledge and experiences, and this association, which now has more than 24,000 members and a national headquarters with 100 employees, has been the most important single force in stimulating the public library movement in the United States. Through the work of its staff and through its Publishing Department, but chiefly through the work of its members, in committees and at meetings, the association has set goals and standards and aroused public support for libraries, benefiting every public library in the country. I can mention only a few of these.

From time to time the Association has adopted standards for public library service which individual libraries and communities could use as a measuring stick to evaluate their own services and in formulating plans for improvement. The most recent standards for public library service were published in 1956. They consist of some seventy guiding principles beginning with "Public library service should be universally available". This general statement is designed to arouse the people without library service by assuring them that free and universal provision for library service is in keeping with the ideal of equal opportunity for every individual. It is followed by an explanation of the possibility of small libraries working together in joint and cooperative programs and of every library being a part of a larger system of libraries. Such systems bring the resources of the largest libraries to all the people. The standards recognize that a community with a population of less than 5000 cannot support an adequate library with a professional librarian, but they insist that even these small libraries should have close and regular guidance by professional personnel. The emphasis on systems of libraries makes these standards applicable to libraries of all sizes. Another key statement in the standards is that "in each state a program of supplementary library service must be maintained at the state level to back up separate libraries and library systems throughout the state". This statement is followed by 15 specific services that the state library agency should perform. All of our 50 states do have library agencies within the state government, but few of them provide all of the services which are enumerated to establish standards of service. Other statements set standards on the kinds of service that should be provided, hours of service, and the frequency of bookmobile stops. In respect to bookmobile stops, the standard says that the intervals should be no greater than two weeks. The size and content of the book collection are also covered in these standards. For example, "The library collection should contain opposing views on controversial topics of interest to the people". The standards provide guidance on the number and qualifications of personnel (at least one staff member for each 2500 people in the service area) and on the organization and control of materials. (Here it is recognized that procedures will differ according to need and circumstance, but that "orderly location with maximum flexibility and availability" should be the goal.) On physical facilities, the standards emphasize that "a library is not a building, but a service organization"; the facilities should fit the program of service, be inviting and easy to use, maintain the highest standards for lighting, and be located so as to provide maximum availability.

Many communities have libraries that exceed the standards. What the Association has done in adopting these statements as standards is to define minimum adequacy of library facilities. The standards establish a base line of service to which the people in every community are entitled.

Another activity of the American Library Association that has been particularly effective in promoting the development of public libraries is its legislative activity, especially at the national level. The Association's headquarters are in the middle of the country, in Chicago, but it has a Washington office where one librarian and her secretary serve as a liaison between libraries and librarians, on the one hand, and the United States Congress, on the other hand. Largely through the work of this office, but with magnificent support from librarians and friends of libraries throughout the country, federal funds have been made available since 1956 to stimulate library development in rural areas. The funds have been too small for the job that needs to be done but they have served, as intended, as seed money, to stimulate local support. In the first three years that federal money has been available to supplement state appropriations for library support, 30 million rural people received new or improved public library services. The money appropriated by the states for rural libraries increased 54 per cent, and local appropriations for libraries in rural areas increased 45 per cent. Approximately 200 new bookmobiles were put into service on rural roads to bring books and information to people in remote areas. And more than 5 million more books were made available to our rural people. These books and services are satisfying a tremendous hunger of young and old. I like the comment of one older man who said, "It is almost too much for me. When I look at all these books of knowledge and adventure at my fingertips and think of how old I am and of how much I've missed in the past, I'm just desperate to know where to begin".

The Association has been instrumental in too many other ways for me to explain them all but I must mention three of them briefly. These are:

1. Encouragement of local and national activities on the part of library trustees and friends of libraries. More than 2000 trustees of

D

public libraries are members of the American Library Association. They have their own organization and programs within the association. Many libraries have organized local groups of laymen as "Friends of the Public Library". Through these groups their members enjoy the association of people having similar interests, and they support the library in many ways, chiefly, I suppose, by the moral support they provide in the community.

2. Continuous public relations activities to make the importance of public library service better known. These activities have great variety. The most spectacular one has been the Association's sponsorship with the National Book Committee, during the last three years, of National Library Week. The National Book Committee is an organization of approximately 100 leading citizens who believe in wider and wiser reading. They have been lending support to libraries by sponsoring a special campaign each spring to make the American people more library conscious. During National Library Week, newspapers, magazines, radio, and television have been persuaded to feature the importance of books and reading. And almost every public library in the United States has capitalized on the nation-wide publicity by local events (exhibits, lectures, open-house receptions, etc.) held at the same time.

3. A national recruiting program to attract able young people to the library profession. There is a great shortage of librarians in the United States which is intensified by expanding library services, and the Association is working actively on this problem.

Perhaps one of the greatest contributions of the American Library Association is its provision of a means for the profession to discuss its problems and its objectives, to formulate its goals and its beliefs and to publicize them in order to support the work of individual librarians wherever they may be. In addition to the standards for public libraries already mentioned, I am thinking of two powerful statements adopted by the Association to express its beliefs: "The Library Bill of Rights" and the "Freedom to Read". The first one, the Library Bill of Rights was adopted twelve years ago to strengthen the hand of every librarian who needed support in order to put his beliefs into practice. It expresses so well the philosophy of librarianship in the United States that I am going to quote it in full. The Association declared that the following five basic policies should govern the services of all libraries.

"1. As a responsibility of library service, books and other reading matter selected should be chosen for values of interest, information and enlightenment of all the people of the community. In no case should any book be excluded because of the race or nationality, or the political or religious views of the writer.

"2. There should be the fullest practicable provision of material presenting all points of view concerning the problems and issues of our times, international, national, and local; and books or other reading matter of sound factual authority should not be proscribed or removed from library shelves because of partisan or doctrinal disapproval.

"3. Censorship of books, urged or practised by volunteer arbiters of morals or political opinion or by organizations that would establish a coercive concept of Americanism, must be challenged by libraries in maintenance of their responsibility to provide public information and enlightenment through the printed word.

"4. Libraries should enlist the cooperation of allied groups in the fields of science, of education, and of book publishing in resisting all abridgment of the free access to ideas and full freedom of expression that are the tradition and heritage of Americans.

"5. As an institution of education for democratic living, the library should welcome the use of its meeting rooms for socially useful and cultural activities and discussion of current public questions. Such meeting places should be available on equal terms to all groups in the community regardless of the beliefs and affiliations of their members."

Couple this pronouncement with the Freedom to Read statement, which was prepared by the American Library Association in cooperation with the American Book Publishers Council in 1953, and you will have insight into the importance of a professional library association in the life of a country. The latter statement begins "The freedom to read is essential to our democracy". This is the beginning of an eloquent statement on censorship of books which was issued to support individual librarians, wherever they might be, if their belief in the necessity of providing books on all sides of controversial questions or representing unpopular points of view should be challenged. "We believe that free communication is essential to the preservation of a free society and a creative culture." These words can as well be applied to the necessity to provide public library service to all the people. Insistence on the right of the people to the freedom to read stakes out a lofty claim for the value of books; at the same time it takes for granted that books will be available. The American public library feels a civic responsibility to make the "freedom to read" meaningful.

5. ACADEMIC AND RESEARCH LIBRARIES IN THE UNITED STATES

LUCILE M. MORSCH

Library of Congress, Washington

LIBRARY services in support of formal education and research is a broad topic. Education is a full-time occupation for approximately one third of all Americans between the age of five and the age of retirement, and more than a billion dollars are being spent annually for research. Recent statistics from the National Science Foundation report a rough estimate of a billion dollars as the amount being spent for basic research in science alone. If the library is really the heart of a school, and library services are indispensable to research, it is obvious that libraries in schools, colleges, universities, and research institutions not related to universities must play an important role in the life of the nation.

To understand the function of academic libraries, one must first have an understanding of the educational system they are to serve. It is not easy, however, to explain a "system" that has as much diversity as ours does. In the United States, education is within the prerogatives of the individual states; there is no central administrative authority to prescribe the organization and aims of education and educational standards, such as is found in most other countries. It is true that we have an Office of Education in the Department of Health, Education, and Welfare, of the Federal Government, but it has no such power; it was created "to collect such statistics and facts as shall show the condition and progress of education, to diffuse such information as shall aid the people of the United States, in the establishment and maintenance of efficient school systems, and otherwise to promote the cause of education".

The state governments are the ones that pass the school laws and set most of the standards; they determine the number of days the schools must be open each year, and prescribe the age limit for compulsory attendance. All of our states have compulsory education laws. The age when children are required to begin school varies in the different states —it may be six, seven or eight years—and the age which they must pass before they can leave school ranges from sixteen to eighteen. This explains, in part, why ninety per cent of American youth between fourteen and eighteen years of age are in school. Diversity in the school system is to be found, moreover, within the various states, because the state superintendents of instruction neither operate the schools nor dictate how they should be run. Local school districts, each with a board of education consisting of (generally) elected members, are given the responsibility for running the school or schools in their area. Nevertheless, there are great similarities, owing to three primary conditions. These are, first, a common belief in the importance of education, which is strengthened by the recognition of the part that schools play in preparing citizens to meet their responsibilities and to understand the economic, political, social, and cultural complexities of modern life. This means the development of a school system with the ideal of equal educational opportunity for all. Second, similarities exist because we are a mobile people, as any cursory study of our population trends will demonstrate, and teachers are a particularly mobile segment of the population. Third, we have many strong professional organizations and many journals in the field of education which facilitate communication and discussion of ideas relating to teaching and the schools.

Schools in the United States are generally classed in three groups, for elementary, secondary, and higher education. The elementary and secondary schools together almost always comprise twelve years of schooling, either with eight years in an elementary school and four in high school, or with six in elementary, three in a junior high school, and three in high school. The 6–3–3 pattern is now most common in the larger urban communities. Higher education is offered by the colleges and universities. The difference between a college and a university is confused by the fact that some institutions with the characteristics of a university are called colleges, and a few colleges and universities are called "institutes". Generally speaking, however, a college offers a four-year course leading to a bachelor's degree and does not have professional schools or graduate courses leading to the master's degree or the doctorate. There are also many junior colleges with a two-year course equal to the first two years of college. A university comprises a college of liberal arts and sciences, as well as professional schools and a graduate college or school which provides programs for study and research beyond the level of the baccalaureate or bachelor's degree. College students are known as "undergraduates", those above the college level are "graduate" students.

Library service in educational institutions begins with the elementary schools; their students are from 6 to 12, or from 6 to 14 years old. Boys and girls study together, and, in most elementary schools, they have the same teacher throughout the day. I wish that I could tell you that every one of these schools has a library in it, but this would be describing a dream as a fact. Nevertheless, we are making much progress towards the realization of this goal. Approximately 30 per cent of the elementary schools have a centralized library; that is to say, they have a library administered as a unit, located in one place, where books are available to all pupils and teachers of the school. Some 50 per cent have classroom collections for the pupils, that is, groups of library books permanently housed in the individual classrooms and not administered from a centralized library. Some other schools are served by collections borrowed from public libraries. Only 3·5 per cent of the elementary schools are reported as having no library facilities. In recent years there has been a growing realization of the importance of school libraries as a rich source of reading material in the development of interests, of habits of creative thinking, and in the skill of reading.

In our high schools, the situation is much better. Approximately 96 per cent of our secondary schools have centralized libraries, but in half of them, the "librarian"—or a teacher who serves also as the librarian—does not have the professional training that a good school library requires. No collection of books deserves to be called a library unless it is used, and the best school libraries are those that are directed by a librarian trained in the particular skills of service to children and young people. The services of a school library are directed first towards enrichment of classroom teaching. This means that the librarian works closely with the teachers to provide books and pamphlets, periodicals and newspapers, maps and pictures, films and filmstrips, and even three-dimensional objects that will make the teaching more vivid and interesting. Permission is generally given to the pupils to spend a certain period each week during the regular school hours in the library in order to help them develop their individual interests, either in subjects to which their classes have introduced them, or simply in "free" reading. "Free" reading means the reading that children choose to do on their own, without suggestion from anyone else. The librarian has the responsibility to open the doors for the pupils to the world of books. He (or more often "she", since most of our school librarians are women) tries to help each child as an individual to find the books best suited to his abilities and his interests. The library provides story hours for small children, book talks and discussions about books for the older ones, book displays and exhibits, and lends books from the school library for reading at home. Teaching the use of the library is also a function of the school library, equally important to the student who does not plan to continue his education beyond high school and to the student who plans to go to college. The former, if his habit of reading is developed, will make use of this skill in using his public library. The latter will be expected to know how to use a library when he enters college. Today, we are told, one out of every three young people graduating from high school attends college.

The functions of a college library are simply an extension of those of the school library, and the student who has had the advantage of a good school library makes the transition with much greater ease than one who has not. He knows the general arrangement of books, because, almost without exception, our academic libraries arrange them by subject either according to the Dewey Decimal Classification, or the Library of Congress Classification. The user is expected to be able to find his own books with little assistance; he knows how to use the library catalogs, because the same general principle of listing the books according to their authors and their titles and the subjects with which they deal, is followed in most American libraries of any type. He knows how to use the periodical indexes, the encyclopedias, and other reference books that will unlock the treasures of the library for him. In college, the student is expected to do independent reading and investigation that requires him to know how to make the best use of the library.

In referring to the fact that our academic libraries are commonly arranged by the Dewey Decimal or the LC classification schemes, and that alphabetical catalogs are available in libraries of every type to make the collections accessible by author, title, and subject, a word of explanation may be helpful. The manner of arranging books necessarily varies among our libraries, because of the consensus that as many books as possible should be displayed, so as to permit the reader to browse at the bookshelves and in the bookstacks and to select those materials that best meet his needs or that attract his interest. Variations in shelving facilities from library to library, whenever the collection has outgrown a single room, will affect this display. If browsing is to be meaningful, some subject arrangement is essential. Whether a library uses one of the two best-known systems, or a combination of the two, or some other classification is not a matter of concern. For example, a library may use the simpler Decimal Classification except for a large, special collection of music which it has classified according to the LC system. Each library maintains a catalog of its collection arranged in the same order as the books on the shelves are arranged. This catalog, known as the "shelf list", is a systematic catalog, but in most libraries it is little used except by the library staff; it shows the relative strengths and weaknesses of the collection by subject and serves as an inventory control and for other administrative purposes. Most readers seem to prefer to consult the books themselves in systematic order rather than to use a systematic catalog.

The catalog approach to subjects is, therefore, an alphabetical one by specific subject headings. It supplements the systematic arrangement of the books. The list of headings used by the Library of Congress serves as the standard list for most libraries; many smaller libraries—public or school—however, use the Sears *List of Subject Headings* (published by the

H. W. Wilson Company) which is based on the Library of Congress list. Most of our library catalogs contain author, title, and subject cards in a single alphabet; catalogs so arranged are known as "dictionary catalogs". In recent years a few libraries have divided their catalogs into two parts, one containing the author and title entries and the other containing the subject entries. The change has seldom been considered wholly advantageous, and the dictionary catalog still reigns supreme in most American libraries.

If his college is a part of one of our very large universities the student usually will require additional instruction in the use of the library. This instruction is more often provided by the professional library staff in formal classes or in an informal introduction in the library, or both. In recent years, separate libraries for the undergraduate students have been developed, with selected book stocks that can be made easily accessible to the students. Even in large institutions, with thousands of students, the librarian is concerned with service directed to the needs of individual professors and students.

The conception of the library as a central force in a university has developed steadily with the growth of the universities. For the better part of a century we have referred to the library as a vital organ, the heart, of a university. Two functions of the library have been emphasized: the storehouse function and the workshop, or laboratory, function. The first of these, the storehouse function, has been recognized, of course, as long as libraries have been in existence. To accumulate and preserve the recorded knowledge of the past and the present is no longer considered enough, however; books must be used to the largest extent possible, and with the least trouble. To make its books useful, the college or university library must regard them primarily as tools rather than treasures. This concept explains the function of an academic library as a workshop. It means that the book collections must support the objectives of the institution of which the library is a part, objectives relating to instruction, to research, to publication, and to the institution's efforts to provide services, beyond its own walls, to its community or to the nation. College and university curricula and research programs and services change with the needs and demands of the times, and the libraries must adjust their services accordingly.

The phenomenal growth of universities and the expansion of their graduate and professional schools has been shared by the university libraries. This growth of library resources has been one of the most pronounced aspects of university development. Many university libraries have quadrupled in the last half century and some have increased tenfold or more. A recent tabulation of statistics for 42 university libraries shows that their book collections range in size from 440,000 to well over six million volumes; 21 of them, or exactly half of the libraries included, contain over a million volumes.

In spite of these developments, no library can hope to be comprehensive and acquire all of the literature of our rapidly-shrinking world to meet the needs of today, to say nothing of anticipating the needs of the future. As a result, university and other research libraries have been forced to emphasize selected fields of knowledge and to share their materials with other institutions. An impressive number of cooperative arrangements have been undertaken by American research libraries and many of these have become standard procedures in library administration.

Cooperation in the development of American library resources led to the creation of the Farmington Plan. Under this arrangement some 60 research libraries have accepted individual responsibilities for collecting the literature of particular subject areas, in order to increase the nation's total resources for research. Ideally—if the Plan could be extended to the literature of all countries and all types of publications, and if it could be made fully effective—it would insure that at least one copy of each new foreign publication that might reasonably be expected to interest a research worker in the United States would be acquired by an American library. Two distinct procedures have been established in the Farmington Plan. In one of these, each participating library has assumed the responsibility for particular subjects. A book dealer in each country of Western Europe, Australia, Mexico, and South Africa has been instructed to obtain a copy of each new book published in his country that falls within the scope of the Plan and to send it to the library responsible for its subject. Books from some other countries, particularly those having languages that few American libraries are prepared to handle, are assigned on an area basis. In these cases, a single library takes responsibility for obtaining all publications of a country, and makes its own arrangements for their acquisition. Each library participating in the program is under obligation to catalog the books received and to send the entries to the National Union Catalog at the Library of Congress, in order to make the books available to other libraries through interlibrary loan.

No less important than continuing cooperative acquisitions programs, such as the Farmington Plan, are one-time cooperative projects. These include the sharing by several libraries of the expenses of an acquisitions librarian on a buying trip to foreign countries, and cooperative microfilming projects. For example, three university libraries and the Library of Congress arranged last year to send a librarian to several countries in Latin America to purchase materials that each one needed, to find out what additional materials in specific subject fields were available, and to make the acquaintance of reliable dealers with whom the libraries could deal in the future. Cooperative microfilming projects make it possible for several, and sometimes many, libraries to share the cost of making a negative, from which positive copies can be made at relatively small cost for each library participating in the project. This is done when none of the libraries has the original, e.g., a rare book in the Bibliothèque Nationale in Paris, or when one American library has a book that other libraries need, but cannot purchase. The same method may be followed when all of the libraries have the original material, but they feel the need to own a microfilm copy, perhaps because the paper is deteriorating, or because they cannot afford to bind and house the original. This is often the case with long runs of newspapers.

Cooperative acquisition may even result in joint ownership. The Midwest Interlibrary Center in Chicago is a cooperative storehouse that belongs to a group of university libraries within a radius of a few hundred miles from Chicago. It was established eleven years ago to permit these libraries to remove from their crowded shelves books that were potentially valuable for research but that were used so infrequently that one copy could serve all the libraries if it were available to them on 24 hours' notice. The idea has worked out so well that now the central collection consists not only of books and journals and documents that have been withdrawn from the members libraries' collections, but also of little-used research materials acquired directly for the Center for the benefit of all of the member libraries.

Another cooperative program for the development of the book collections of American libraries is based on the fact that every library receives duplicates that it does not need and can profitably exchange with another library for books that it does need. The program is operated by a private, non-profit corporation by the name of the United States Book Exchange (USBE) which handles the exchange of surplus duplicates between libraries. It is sponsored by the various national library associations; the American Library Association, the Special Libraries Association, the Medical Library Association, etc., and by the American Council of Learned Societies and the National Research Council. Libraries, in addition to duplicates, use for exchange purposes their own publications and the publications of the institutions of which they are a part. To overcome the difficulty of knowing which library may need its surplus books, or where it can locate a volume to fill the gap in an incomplete set, a library by becoming a member of the United States Book Exchange, can easily dispose of its surplus books; it sends them to this central pool, and is then eligible to draw on the collection for other books. One of the purposes of establishing the United States Book Exchange was to facilitate international exchange which is particularly difficult. The Exchange now has more than 2300 members, and approximately 54 per cent of these are outside the United States. The expansion of curricula in recent years in many universities, to say nothing of the establishment of many new universities, has often made it necessary to build up a basic book collection starting from nothing. To locate out-of-print books through the regular book trade is usually prohibitively expensive in such cases, and many books are simply not available through this means. To join the USBE a library merely indicates that it has material that it can send to the center, and that it wishes to be a member. It then pays the shipping costs of the books it sends and of those it receives and a modest service fee for each piece that it acquires.

The earliest major cooperative undertaking of American research libraries was in the field of cooperative cataloging. Before the turn of this century the Library of Congress began to print its catalog cards and to offer copies of them to other libraries for a few cents each. The other libraries buy copies of the printed card instead of making their own for those books which they acquire for their own collections. Shortly after it initiated this card printing, the Library of Congress also began to print cards for books in the library of the United States Department of Agriculture, and sold these on the same basis. The Department of Agriculture cataloged its books that were not in the Library of Congress, and sent the entry to the Library of Congress for printing. Other Federal government libraries and, later, university and public libraries followed, and the program continued to grow, until most of the great libraries in the United States had joined the program. Now the cooperative cataloging program is not limited to books which are not in the Library of Congress. If a library orders cards for a book which the national library has not yet acquired, it may be requested to supply copy for printing, so that cards will be made available as soon as possible for any other library that needs them. The Library of Congress is proud of its catalog card service, augmented through cooperative cataloging, because it provides a substantial service to all libraries. Most of the libraries in the United States and many libraries abroad subscribe to this service; approximately 32 million cards are being sold annually to some 10,000 subscribers. These cards are printed not only for books and pamphlets, but for publications of all kinds: government documents, reports, periodicals, music, phonograph records, books for the blind, maps, microfilms, motion pictures, and filmstrips. Since the Library's printing facilities include Greek, Gaelic, Hebrew, Arabic, and Cyrillic type, and the Library reproduces characters employed by the languages of the Far East by photographic methods, the cards for books in these languages are of particular importance to research libraries which lack these facilities and which do not command a staff of catalogers competent in all of these languages.

To appreciate the value of these cards to other libraries and hence to the scholarly world, one needs to recognize that in addition to linguistic competence, the catalogers must have expert knowledge of the various subject fields and expert technical competence in cataloging and classifying. The Library of Congress cataloging staff is large enough to permit subject or language specialization and has at hand for its work an unexcelled reference collection of general and special biographical, bibliographical, and encyclopedic publications.

Looking at American academic and research libraries as a whole, one sees a unifying effect from the wide use of Library of Congress printed catalog cards. A scholar in any of our libraries is most likely to find that its basic catalog consists largely of these cards which are designed to be filed according to the authors, the titles, and the subjects with which the books deal, all in a single alphabet. Standardization of bibliographic citations is also a corollary of the general use of the printed card service.

Another example of a major cooperative undertaking of American research libraries is the National Union Catalog in the Library of Congress. It was begun more than thirty years ago and now contains some 15 million cards contributed by more than 2000 libraries in the United States and Canada. It has proved invaluable in identifying and locating copies of books for interlibrary loan and for other bibliographic purposes. Since 1956 the Library of Congress has been publishing as additions to its own catalog in book form, titles published in 1956 or later and reported to the National Union Catalog by the libraries owning them; symbols indicate the libraries in which they may be found. This catalog is published monthly and is cumulated quarterly, annually, and at five-year intervals. Additions continue to be made to the card catalog as titles published before 1956 are reported.

Numerous other catalogs and lists, some of national scope, some regional or local, have been created through cooperative effort. Among the most notable have been union lists of serials, of American newspapers, of serial publications of foreign governments, and of microfilms, a census of medieval and renaissance manuscripts, and several censuses of fifteenth century books in the United States. Three monthly, cumulative publications currently being issued by the Library of Congress are the product of nation-wide cooperation. *New Serial Titles* reports the holdings in several hundred libraries of periodicals and other serial publications which started publication since the great *Union List of Serials* and its supplements appeared. Approximately 200 libraries report their receipts of books and periodicals in the Russian language to the *Monthly Index of Russian Accessions*, and contribute to the publication of the *East European Accessions Index* by similarly reporting the literature from ten countries of Eastern Europe.

From the foregoing it should be apparent that the Library of Congress is the leading research library in the United States. Even without being the national library in name, it provides the services of a national library, and other United States libraries look to it for leadership. Its vast collections, containing approximately 12 million volumes (totalling nearly 39 million pieces, when one counts maps, phonograph records, bound volumes of newspapers, manuscripts, fine prints and photographs, microfilms, etc.) supplement the collections of other libraries. As a national library, the Library of Congress represents the United States for the international exchange of government publications, and it has the benefit of assistance from the Department of State in working out some exchange agreements with other countries. The Copyright Office of the United States is a department of the Library, and, although an inclusive *dépôt légal* is unknown in the United States, we do have a deposit system for those publications and unpublished works for which copyright protection is sought. Thus most of the major publications issued in the United States (with the exception of government publications) and a considerable number published in other countries, are deposited with the Register of Copyrights. The Copyright Office was made a part of the Library of Congress in order that the books deposited in it would be available for the enrichment of the Library; it is, however, an office of record only, and the Library is not under obligation to retain permanently any deposited materials it does not want. The Library's Selection Officer examines the copyright receipts every day, selects from them everything of research value, and rejects the rest.

The rich and extensive collections of the Library of Congress are too vast to be described briefly. Suffice it to say that they offer opportunities for almost unlimited research which supplement those of all the other research libraries in the country. The Music Division, for example, is a special library within the Library of Congress which contains probably the most comprehensive collection of music and the literature of music that has ever been assembled. The collection represents the art of music—written, printed, and phonographically recorded—in its every aspect, and contains voluminous writings about music produced over the centuries by philosophers, historians, critics, and other scholars. The Law Library of the Library of Congress also has a comprehensive collection; it contains works of every age and system of law from ancient times to the present, from the Far East to the Far West. In addition to rare books in the Music Division and the Law Library, the Library of Congress has a Rare Book Division containing some 250,000 books. These include almost 5600 incunabula, books printed in the Western World before the year 1501.

The resources of the Library of Congress are particularly important for research in American history and politics. The Library has long held that it should possess all books and other materials (whether in original or in copy) which express and record the life and achievements of the people of the United States. In addition to the collections of published materials, the Library has more than 16 million manuscripts and reproductions thereof relating to American history and civilization. These manuscripts are chiefly the personal papers—correspondence, journals, diaries, and unpublished writings of any kind—of individuals who have been important in the history of the United States: statesmen, political figures, military leaders, scientists, philanthropists, etc.

The Library's collections in science and technology, distinguished for almost a century, consist of more than 1,500,000 volumes and are supplemented by the collections in the National Library of Medicine and the Library of the United States Department of Agriculture. Both of these other libraries are recognized as national libraries, and the Library of Congress strives to prevent unnecessary duplication of their collections by refraining from purchasing books in the fields of technical agriculture and clinical medicine.

There are approximately 130 special libraries in the Federal Government in Washington; many of them have research collections which compare favorably with the outstanding research libraries of the world in their fields. These libraries exist primarily for the benefit of the agencies of the Government of which they are a part; most of them, however, are open to the public, and, almost without exception, they participate in interlibrary loan. Many of these libraries weed their collections periodically, and transfer to the Library of Congress those volumes that are no longer needed often enough to justify their retention. Occasional needs later can be satisfied by borrowing the volume from the Library of Congress. Through transfers and interlibrary loans, such as those briefly described here, the entire resources of the libraries, in the Federal Government, are made available to the scholarly community.

The Library of Congress also lends books to other libraries, both in the United States and abroad, if sending them out of the city will not interfere with service to the Congress and to the Government. It also serves as a channel for requests from foreign libraries that wish to borrow a book from an American library but do not know where it may be available. The Library of Congress either lends the book itself or refers the request to another library willing to lend books abroad.

Research workers and others may acquire copies of material in the Library of Congress. A fully-equipped photographic laboratory, operated on a fee basis, with a staff of 90, makes microfilm, Photostat, or Xerox copies of materials in the Library, unless copyright or other restrictions prevent copying.

Libraries and individuals who do not need the books or other materials in the Library of Congress still benefit from its many services. Among them are the regular monthly publication of catalogs, checklists, and indexes. Numerous bibliographies and technical library publications, such as classification schedules and cataloging rules, are issued by the Library. The Library publishes occasional lectures delivered at the Library, and issues phonograph records from its Archive of Folk Song or its Archive of Recorded Poetry and Literature. Persons in Washington —both residents and the hundreds of thousands of visitors who come to the Nation's capital each year—may take advantage of the many exhibits that are presented in the Library to display the Library's treasures of books, manuscripts, photographs, and fine prints, and the print show that is an annual event in the Library, and they may attend chamber music concerts, poetry readings and literary lectures by poets and other writers that are presented in its auditorium. The generosity of several patrons of music, literature, and the arts who have endowed the Library make such events possible.

There is a real temptation to elaborate further on the Library of Congress, but I do not wish to overemphasize it, in an account of academic and research libraries in the United States. Rather, I want to show that it is an integral part of a vast network of research libraries, and that it plays an active role, not only in supplementing their collections, but in actually increasing the number and variety of services which they can provide to their local clientele. Because of the participation of the Library of Congress in many cooperative programs, because of its continuing leadership, and because its rich collections and the fruits of the work of its large, specialized, professionally-competent staff are made available not only to scholars and research workers, but on a large scale to other libraries, all libraries throughout the world are the richer.

It should be emphasized that even though the Library of Congress deserves great credit for many of the projects I have described, few of them could have been accomplished without the cooperation of other research libraries. In fact, sometimes such projects originate with other libraries or in the library organizations, such as the Association of Research Libraries and the Library of Congress is persuaded to carry them out.

The Library of Congress shares many problems with other large libraries and seeks every opportunity to encourage or engage in research to solve them. The amount of research into library problems seems to be increasing, but the consensus is that the problems that need serious study are probably increasing at a greater rate. Perhaps it is, rather, that librarians have become more aware of problems that are not new. An occasional publication entitled *Library Research in Progress* is issued by the Library Services Branch in the United States Office of Education. The four issues which have so far appeared list 239 projects underway. Some substantial research is performed by individual librarians as a labor of love, but in general an employed librarian has great difficulty in finding enough free time to make this possible. The doctoral program in our library schools deserves credit for much of the increase in research in this field, because if its emphasis on research methods and its requirement of a dissertation based upon research.

The greatest stimulation to research into library problems came in 1956 when the Council on Library Resources, Inc., was established to administer a grant of $5 million from the Ford Foundation, to be expended over a five-year period. The principal objective of this new foundation is to aid in the solution of library problems and, specifically, to improve methods of acquiring, storing, organizing, retrieving, reproducing, and transmitting information in libraries. The Council is, therefore interested in increasing the effectiveness of the conventional techniques employed in libraries and in applying newly-developed knowledge, ideas, and methods, including technology, to library work. At first, it was feared that the Council was only going to interest itself in the use of machines and gadgets in libraries but this has not turned out to be the case. Grants have been made to individuals, to libraries, to research organizations, and to library associations, to study a wide range of problems: among others, paper deterioration; problems related to the selection, acquisition, and cataloging of books; the standardization and testing of library equipment and supplies; and circulation systems. The possibilities of more effective use of mechanical devices have not been neglected. Studies have included an experiment involving the use of closed-circuit television in a university library to permit a professor to consult in his departmental library materials located in the central library; this experiment led to two grants from the Council for investigation of a more satisfactory, automatic page turner than had been available. Another study related to the mechanization of bibliographic compilation and publication. Still another related to an inexpensive, instant-copy camera for the special use of catalogers.

The unsolved problems of academic and research libraries are numerous and difficult. They deal with both the present and future effectiveness with which libraries perform their functions. Because they are sufficiently challenging to engage the best minds, the library profession is never dull for anyone who gets involved in trying to solve them.

6. BOOKS AND LIBRARIES IN OUR TIME II:
INTRODUCTION OF THE SECOND LECTURER

PROF. BEDRETTIN TUNCEL
Minister of Education, Turkey

THE Turkish people are in this generation called upon to deal with complicated problems which face all populous nations where the people seek to develop their higher powers and to achieve their share of happiness and security. These problems are being faced by the Turkish people and their leaders with courage and determination. There are great tasks of education and of public leadership which lie ahead of us if Turkey is to cultivate the higher powers of her people and give them more of the good things which are today within their reach. The achieving of these things will require us, as other modern nations, to have access to the best thought and experience of all other nations. No nation lives any longer in isolation. Each nation needs the stimulus of the works of the creative imagination of others; and in science and technology, we have reached the point where the total sum of knowledge already accumulated, and every day rapidly accumulating, is so great that any people is sure to fall behind which does not keep abreast of what others are doing. To afford access to the fruits of the intellectual efforts of all nations in all fields, well-equipped libraries and good librarians have become a modern necessity.

The development of library science in Turkey, on a level commensurate with its growing importance in modern life, will require in Turkey as elsewhere the efforts of many people—professors, writers, the entire educated leadership of the country. But it requires also the systematic attention of professors and students of library science. The Faculty of Letters has wisely taken the initiative in organizing work in this field. The Institute began as a center of instruction and this step has proved a wise one. More recently, the Faculty created a Chair of Library Science and we have begun to see evidences of a determination to discharge fully the responsibilities of a Chair. This Series, which is bringing carefully selected specialists to Turkey, is an example. By drawing on competent thinkers and providing further stimulus to thought on problems of importance, the Series provides a precedent which may have uses in other fields.

Public attention to the development of libraries is particularly important at this time. At no other period in our history has the need been greater for wise decisions by the people themselves on problems concerning their future. All Turkey is interested in promoting popular enlightenment as a means of equipping ourselves to decide matters which are the responsibility of a self-governing people. It is important to remember that the library is a great instrument of education, and it belongs inside not outside national plans for raising, as we hope to do, the general level of popular enlightenment.

The speaker who continues the series this afternoon, Mr. Lionel McColvin, is here to analyze and interpret the library experience of Great Britain. Mr. McColvin has been Librarian of the City of Westminster Public Libraries since 1938, and prior to that date was in charge of large libraries in London and elsewhere. He has travelled widely, having visited the United States, Australia, New Zealand, Germany, the Middle East, and Norway and Sweden, studying library administration in those countries. He holds many important honorary appointments, in particular being President of the Society of Municipal and County Chief Librarians and Vice-President of the International Federation of Library Associations, and serves on the Executive Committees of various bodies such as the National Central Library, UNESCO, the Central Music Library, etc. In 1952 he was the President of the Library Association. In addition, he is the author of several books covering various aspects of libraries and librarianship. Turkey greets Mr. McColvin with pleasure, and I now invite him to present his lecture.

7. THE BRITISH PUBLIC LIBRARY

LIONEL McCOLVIN

City of Westminster Public Libraries, London

ALTHOUGH I have been asked to deal with all the different types of library service that are provided in Great Britain, I propose to deal first with the public library service, not only because this is the branch of librarianship in which I have spent my own life but also because probably it is in the public library service that provision in different countries shows most difference. In broad essentials the national and university and other libraries of learning and the more modern libraries of scientific research are very similar to one another throughout the world, but there seem to be many different ways of providing library services to the general public, and it is here that even now one country has most to show to another.

In Great Britain the public library service has been developing much on its present lines for over a hundred years. Before then library provision was very limited. We had—as had most countries—our libraries of learning dating back to the Middle Ages when the libraries of monasteries and cathedrals and of our first universities were established. For centuries these were, with the libraries of our more important colleges and grammar schools, practically the only libraries in the country. Only a few people could read or had any interest in literature excepting the literature of the stage.

In the eighteenth century, however, more and more people became interested in reading, particularly people of what we used to call the "middle classes", that is to say the professional men, tradespeople and others who were able to afford to have their sons and daughters educated. These people were particularly concerned in books as a very interesting and enjoyable recreation and libraries sprang up throughout the country to meet this new demand. These libraries were of two main kinds. Some of them were subscription libraries which were organized by the would-be readers who each paid an annual subscription which was spent to provide books to be lent among the members of the Society. Some of these libraries still exist, although many of them died in face of the competition of the better equipped public library. The second type of library was the commercial lending library, the first being started by booksellers who lent books on payment of a small fee. Libraries of this kind still flourish in this country, though they are now generally interested in the newest novels and biographies of wide general appeal.

One would not find in Great Britain—with one exception—any libraries comparable with the town libraries that were set up during the seventeenth and eighteenth centuries in many cities on the continent of Europe; but a few small collections bought with money given to the town were established at Norwich, Ipswich, Coventry and elsewhere. These libraries soon became unused because there was no money to maintain them and keep them provided regularly with new material. Only one of them, the Chetham Library at Manchester, is still in existence.

It will be quite clear, therefore, that at the beginning of the nineteenth century the ordinary man had little opportunity to read; but at that time there began a growing desire on the part of the working man to educate himself, so that he could take a keener interest and play a greater part in the life of his time. Consequently, when in 1800 a Scottish teacher of Philosophy, George Birkbeck, started classes and a library for the mechanics of that city, his example was followed throughout the country, so that by 1849 there were some 400 of these Mechanics' Institutes as they were called. They were financed, however, solely by the very modest subscriptions of the members, and very soon it became evident that if the general public were to be provided with the opportunity to read, a better financed, more permanent type of library service was necessary.

Then the public library movement came into being. Like many other movements, it owed its existence to the enthusiasm of two or three men. Of these the most influential was a young library assistant at the British Museum called Edward Edwards who, being very critical of the library services then available in London, succeeded in interesting a Member of Parliament called William Ewart, who in 1849 got Parliament to authorize an enquiry into the state of libraries in this country as compared with the facilities available elsewhere in Europe. As a result of this document Ewart was able to persuade Parliament to pass the first Public Libraries Act the following year.

In Great Britain local government is in the hands of elected Councils —for various cities, towns, rural districts and counties—who are responsible for providing a great many local services such as schools, roads, public health facilities and so on. These local councils can only do what they are either told to do or allowed to do by Parliament. The first Public Libraries Act was one which allowed them to provide libraries if they wanted to do so. At first the amount of money they could spend was limited to a very small proportion of the total local taxation. Libraries could only be set up after a vote had been taken of the electors, and, strange though it may seem, none of the money raised by local rates could be spent on buying books. Five years later this Act was revised and permitted the expenditure of a larger amount, the product of a rate of 1d. in the pound, and permitted expenditure on books. This limitation of the amount that a Council could spend remained in force until 1919 and as the amount—always too small—gradually became more and more inadequate, the limitation had a serious effect upon the service, preventing it from undertaking its proper task. I mention this because I think it is very important that in any new library services whoever are responsible for the libraries should be allowed to spend as much as they are willing in order that libraries should be really efficient and well supplied with books and staff.

It must not be supposed that local Councils showed great eagerness to make use of their powers and to set up libraries all over the country. On the contrary, during the first twenty years only 35 places started public library services. The first to do so was Manchester, which employed as its first librarian none other than Edward Edwards. At Manchester Edwards established the general principles of the public library service in this country which have been followed ever since. The most important feature of the British public library service from the very outset is that it must be given freely to any member of the public who wants to use it. The cost of the public library is borne collectively by all those people who pay local taxes—rates as we call them—whether they use the library or not, but the man who wishes to use the library may not be charged any subscription or fee, or be asked to make any other payment in order to enjoy to the full whatever is provided by the library. This I regard as vitally important. I have studied library services in many parts of the world, and know that in some of them the user of the library is required to make a personal payment. I am quite sure that, for a variety of reasons, this is a bad thing to do. For example, the library is, among other things, a vital means of self education; but if a charge is made, those people most in need of the help of a public library are often those who are least willing to pay anything for this opportunity. Again in any community there will always be some few people who cannot reasonably afford to pay even a modest subscription. No less important is the fact that when the users are asked to pay a subscription there is a serious tendency to pay undue attention to the more popular demands of the members. Consequently there is a danger that the library will favour the popular and the trivial at the expense of more serious books which, though they may be needed by only a small minority, are nevertheless of great importance to the individual readers and to the community as a whole. Among other reasons I would mention the fact that where the library is, as in some countries, supported partly by public subscription and partly, and perhaps largely, from local

Council funds, it is not unnatural for the local Council to encourage the Library Committee to increase the subscription income by providing the popular material which will attract the most readers.

The first public libraries, and indeed all public libraries, ever since have been keenly interested in another kind of freedom. The public library being provided by the community as a whole at the expense of the whole community, it has always been regarded as of great importance that the library should offer hospitality to books of all kinds embracing all aspects of opinion. It cannot and does not ever want to take sides, to indulge in propaganda, to favour one kind of religious belief or political faith and to exclude another. It has always been the duty of a public library to provide the individual reader with the opportunity to hear all sides and to read about all things and to make up his own mind what he should believe and what he should prefer. This again is to my mind a fundamental responsibility of those in charge of public library services everywhere.

I do not suggest, of course, that, especially in the early days but even still today, every public library is able to offer its readers all the books that it should make available. The amount of money provided for the purchase of books and for the general management of the library service depends upon the understanding and enthusiasm of the local Council. The British public library service is and always has been entirely a local responsibility. There is no department of the national government which is concerned with public library services. All the money has come from local revenue, with no assistance whatever from national taxation. There is no one, therefore, to tell any local Council how much or how little it should spend or how it should spend the money. The result of this local independence is that today we find a wide variety in the standards of efficiency to be found in different libraries. I shall return to this matter later, because it is one which most librarians today think should be remedied; but one must admit that although local independence can produce apathy and neglect it has also made possible the development of excellent library services by those Councils with sufficient wisdom to recognize their importance.

Earlier I mentioned the fact that in 1919 a new Act of Parliament permitted local Councils to spend as much money as they wished—or as little—on their libraries. It also introduced an important change in the administration of libraries which I may find rather difficult to explain.

In Great Britain there are three kinds of local authorities. There are the Councils of the larger cities which are able to carry out all the duties of local government for their own area. These County Boroughs, as they are called, are the larger cities and towns and are responsible for education, public health, libraries and so on within their own boundaries.

The second type of local authority is the County. All the rest of the country outside the County Boroughs is governed by a number of County Councils and within each county one will find a great variety of other local areas such as the smaller towns, the villages and the country districts. Each of these smaller areas within the county has its own local Council and is responsible for some usually purely local matters. Before 1919 many of these smaller Councils started their own library services but in 1919 the County Council was for the first time given power to provide libraries for all those places inside the county area which had not until then provided libraries and indeed there were hardly any library services available in the rural areas but only in the smaller towns.

From 1919, as I have said, the County Councils secured permission to provide libraries but only for all those places within the county area that had not already established their local library. These towns, some of them with libraries 60 and 70 years old, could remain independent, or if they liked could hand over their powers to the County Council. Very few of them did so, so we now have a very illogical pattern. In every county there are some independent libraries, large or small, and in some counties there have grown up big towns which had no libraries before 1919 and which consequently get their library service from the County Council. I will, however, deal with the problems arising from this position later on.

Although standards vary enormously most public libraries show much the same pattern of library provision. Let us glance first at the town library. There are almost always four main departments. First of all there is the lending department, from which books may be borrowed for home reading; next there is the reference department which provides an information service on all matters required by the public as well as facilities for study on the premises; thirdly, most libraries provide a department in which current periodicals and magazines may be read; and fourthly, many libraries have a separate department for the use of children. In the smaller library, particularly the smaller branch library, these departments may be combined. For example the periodicals and the reference section might occupy one room and the children may have to borrow their books from a part of the adult lending library. In extreme cases, as in a small branch, all these services may be given from one room. On the other hand additional departments and developments will be found in some libraries, mostly those serving larger populations. In all town libraries irrespective of the size of the town, we will find one department: a local collection in which material relating to the history, social and cultural life of the city is collected and preserved. One frequently finds a department specially devoted to science and technology, with an emphasis on the needs of local industry. This may be combined with a special department concerned with business and commerce, or there may be a separate commercial library. At other places one may find special departments devoted, for example, to music, fine arts, gramophone records and so on.

In the smaller more compact towns, one library will suffice and be within reasonable access for all residents, but in the larger towns it becomes necessary to set up branch libraries in addition to a main central library at which probably the more specialized resources will be concentrated. It is the purpose of a branch library to bring the library service within easy reach of all residents. As a general rule it is felt that no one should need to travel more than about one mile to his nearest service point but in the siting of branch libraries many factors must be taken into consideration, such as the local transport facilities and the desirability of putting branch libraries in shopping centres and other places to which people will go for a variety of different reasons. We have found, however, that it is a mistake to have too many branches, because it then becomes expensive and often impossible to maintain a good choice of books and to offer suitable staffing.

The branches are closely linked with the central library. The borrower can always use whichever library he finds most convenient or most suitable, and in addition there are usually arrangements by which books requested by branch readers can be sent for them from the central library or from any other place where they are available. In general, however, the branch library caters for the more popular and less specialized needs and the central library endeavours to offer the widest possible range of materials.

So far as children are concerned most of the work will be done by the branch libraries because it is undesirable to bring children into the busy centre of the town. Indeed in some places there are no facilities for children at the central library, which may be situated in a business area with very few residents.

In the county library area different problems may arise. In most counties there are a number of smaller towns—indeed there are still some quite large towns served by the county service because, as discussed earlier, they had not established their libraries before 1919. In these towns within the county area one will find very much the same kind of service as one would find in independent towns of the same size, that is to say, they will have whole time branches often as big and as well provided as the libraries of independent towns, but the county library has also to serve the people who live in the very small towns, the villages and often in isolated farms and cottages dispersed throughout the countryside.

First let it be said that the country reader is always allowed to use the branch in the town to which he will go to do his shopping and visit the cinema, etc., if it is part of the county system; but it is also important to take books to the homes of readers and especially to the children. Originally the county library worked solely through a large number of what were called "centres". A centre is a place, perhaps only open for two or three hours a week to which very small collections of books were sent from County Headquarters. They are usually looked after by unpaid volunteers and situated in such premises as schools, village clubs, shops, post offices, even in the homes of individual readers. The disadvantages of the centre system soon became clear, chiefly the fact that the readers had access only to a very small selection but also the fact that they had no direct contact with experienced librarians who were able to help them to get the books that they require for their own particular needs. Consequently during the last few years, county libraries have more and more developed a system of travelling libraries. The travelling library, as we use the term, is a specially constructed van which is shelved inside to contain 2000 or more volumes with space for readers to go inside the van as into a small library and choose their books from the open shelves. The van goes around in accordance with a regular programme so that borrowers know exactly when to go to change their books and the van will stay for varying lengths of time, from half an hour to two or three hours, according to the local demands. There is always a trained librarian travelling with the vehicle who can help readers and arrange for their special needs to be met either when the van comes round next or immediately by post. In a great many cases the local centre is still kept open as it supplements the travelling library service and also often provides a local meeting place for people interested in books.

Another interesting development is that of the regional library which is a large county branch serving as a centre for the surrounding country districts. The librarian in charge is responsible for supervising the work done by the smaller branches and centres in his region and a regional library may well act as the Headquarters of one or more travelling libraries.

Before I go any further let me mention something of the utmost importance. Every public library in this country now offers its readers free access to the shelves so that he may see what is available and make his own choice of the books most likely to interest him or meet any special needs. When our public libraries were first started this privilege was not extended to readers, who were expected to choose what they needed from catalogues, and were denied the opportunity to handle and consult the available material. Alas, this system still prevails in many libraries in other countries. I must, however, say most emphatically that it is absolutely essential to give readers this open access service; without it, it is impossible for them to find exactly what they need. Unless they can see the books for themselves they lose all the educational value that comes from contact with the rich variety of material available in the library. And, from a severely practical point of view, if the same number of readers are to borrow the same number of books from any library that does not offer open access, a great many more staff will be needed at greater expense. That, however, is relatively unimportant. What matters is that a public library is a means of educating and enriching the experience of readers and this cannot be done unless readers can handle and choose at their own free will.

It follows, of course, that in an open access library it is essential that the books should be arranged in accordance with a suitable system of classification, so that the reader has before him all the books on the same subject, each subject being in close proximity to related matters.

As I told you earlier, our public libraries have been provided by local councils who have never been compelled to do so. The development of public libraries has, therefore, been made entirely at the free will of the different local councils, and it is a very remarkable thing that the spread of the movement has been such that there is now only one place in Great Britain which does not have its own public library service. Undoubtedly our public libraries are not all good enough, and there are other weaknesses in the system, but I think it is most significant that nation-wide coverage should have been achieved without any kind of compulsion. Here indeed is proof that the public library has become an essential element in the social, educational and cultural life of the modern world.

Thus the whole of the United Kingdom of England, Wales, Scotland, and Northern Ireland is provided with public library services given by 559 independent library authorities, 464 towns and 95 counties. The population served by these independent systems range from under 200 to over one million. Every system has its own main or central library but in addition there are 1,334 whole time branches open at least thirty hours each week and over 31,500 smaller branches and centres open for lesser periods. In addition there are 235 travelling libraries working on the lines already described.

At least every third person in the total population uses his or her public library regularly. About 28 per cent borrow regularly from the lending departments and many others use the reference libraries, magazine rooms and other facilities but don't borrow. Last year, however, nearly 400 million volumes were lent for home reading, an average of about 8 volumes for every member of the total population and an average of 27 for each registered borrower.

Nevertheless, because the outstanding feature of a public library is that it enables people to share the books and other services that are provided, the cost to the individual—his contribution from local rates—is very small. The average expenditure last year on public libraries was no more than 7s. 4d. for a year per head of total population; of this 1s. 9½d. per head was spent on buying books.

Averages can be misleading, however. Some libraries spend a great deal more than average. Excluding three or four libraries in central London where most of the users do not live in the area but work there, 51 libraries had a total expenditure of more than 10s. per head of total population, and 16 spent more than 3s. per head on books. Others spent much less; 8 even had a total expenditure of less than 2s. and 40 spent less than 1s. a year per head on books. Obviously these places must and do have very bad libraries, ill staffed, ill kept, with grossly inadequate book stocks. This serious difference between good and bad is, of course, the result of our system of local independence. Where the council has been keen, where it has had a progressive librarian, the library has had reasonable support. But where the council has not understood the value of the service or has not cared, it has been sadly neglected. The great difference between the good and the bad is a cause for concern among those who are interested in the public library movement. Undoubtedly the residents in bad library areas are seriously deprived of a necessary public service. Commerce, education, culture, and indeed the enjoyment of leisure are prejudiced. Many of us, therefore, wish there was a minister of the national government, with a suitable staff and inspectorate, able to insist upon reasonable standards everywhere. We do not want any system which will interfere with the local administration of libraries or in any way hinder the progressive, or impose standardized methods and provision. The keen progressive councils, eager to experiment, to develop new provisions and methods, have played a great part in the gradual improvement of the public library service and must be able to continue this vital task. Excessive control by a national department concerned with libraries *can*—and in some countries *does*—act like a dead hand, hindering progress, standardizing book supply and methods. Perhaps it is fear of such undesirable interference that has so far kept British library authorities and librarians from seeking the intervention of the national government. However if the dangers are foreseen there is no reason why, again as in some other countries, the national government should not both stimulate progress and insist upon reasonable standards everywhere.

In 1957 our government appointed a committee to consider the future development of public libraries, and one of its recommendations is that our Ministry of Education should have general responsibility for the public library services of local councils, with powers to insist that at least the more backward authorities shall improve their libraries.

Another serious problem with which this committee was concerned was that of the minimum size of the independent library authority. I have explained how our libraries grew up in such a way that places both very large and very small could have their own independent libraries. Consequently very many of them are far too small to do the work properly. No fewer than 163 out of the total of 559 serve populations of fewer than 30,000; of these 116 have fewer than 20,000 inhabitants and 32 fewer than 10,000. These, manifestly, are far too small. To be reasonably efficient a library must be able to afford two things—to provide a sufficient range and variety of books to meet the more usual requirements of a population, each member of which may be interested in one or more subjects in a great range of material—books for education and recreation, works of literature, books on the countries of the world and their history and conditions, on science, technology, commerce, the fine arts, religion, psychology, and many other things—and including books for both adults and children. This book stock must, moreover, be kept up to date, embracing the latest ideas, developments and conditions. And, all the while the book stock gets worn out, becomes out of date and must be replaced and renewed; and, also the number of users steadily increases. The committee, of which I spoke, expressed the firm opinion that no local authority which was not able and willing to spend at least £5000 a year on books alone should continue as an independent service. As they sought to preserve as many independent library authorities as possible provided they reached minimum standards, this figure was definitely the very lowest possible. Any library authority unable or unwilling to reach this absolute minimum should give up its independence and become part of the appropriate county library system.

Another essential of a good public library is staff. At present there are just under 14,000 whole time assistants employed, an average of one for each 3650 of population. It was the view of the committee just mentioned that there should be at least one assistant (excluding the chief librarian) for every 3000 of population served. Of these assistants about 40 per cent should be experienced, professionally qualified librarians. The exact proportion will vary according to local conditions, but the general principle, with which I heartily agree, is that at every branch and every department—adult lending, reference, for children, etc.—there should always be on duty a qualified librarian able to give all necessary help to the public. Larger departments will need more, of course, and, similarly expert assistants are needed in all special departments, such as the commercial, technical, musical and others to which I have referred. I shall deal later with problems of staff training and so on. My point now is that the work of the modern public library demands comprehensive, up-to-date book stocks and qualified staff, and that these are quite beyond the resources of the small independent library. The moral is that if we were starting again, knowing as much as we know now, we would so organize our library service that it was given by authorities big enough and wealthy enough to do the job properly. To start as we did, with too many independent libraries makes it very difficult to bring them together later, because local councils are always, and everywhere, reluctant to relinquish any powers they have once enjoyed, even if they had never used them fully and wisely.

However, I must not finish this lecture on a note of criticism. Perhaps it is because we have already done so much that we understand how much more we should be able to do. I feel it my duty to offer you these two most significant aspects of the public library system in Great Britain. We have gradually built up a system that covers the whole country, that has a firmly established basis of freedom, that has its black spots, but also many public libraries sufficiently good and sufficiently progressive to point clearly to the need for good libraries everywhere, and to indicate the lines on which we must seek nation-wide improvement.

8. THE BRITISH LIBRARY SYSTEM

LIONEL MCCOLVIN

City of Westminster Public Libraries, London

In my previous lecture I spoke chiefly about the British public library system. May I now outline some other types of library provision, show how they are more and more working together in the general interests of readers and conclude with a few words on methods and on the profession of librarian.

Most akin to the public library is the work done for school children. For many years now the public libraries have made special provision for children, including the youngest children as soon as they are able to enjoy picture books and to read simple stories. The majority of libraries provide special departments for children, staffed by assistants who are particularly interested in this work. These children's departments are open after school hours and on days when the schools are closed, including the various holiday periods. We believe that it is important to bring the children to the public library at an early age because then they get into the habit of going to the public library and will be most likely to continue to go there when they leave school. The public library has become an essential part of their life right from the outset.

At the same time there should be suitable libraries in all schools. One often hears discussion as to whether the children should be served by the school or by the public library, but I think this argument is quite unnecessary. There cannot be too many places at which children will be brought into contact with books. It is also important to remember that *all* children go to school and that a keen teacher can make sure that every youngster is told about books and encouraged to read them, whereas the public library can serve only those children who are sufficiently interested and know enough about books to go there. The provision of school libraries has been late in developing. Apart from those at the larger public schools, few useful collections were available until a few years ago when the provision of school libraries in secondary schools became general. Educationists now generally agree that there should be a separate library room in every secondary school and that it should be in charge of a librarian who has had some training and who is allowed sufficient free time to make it fully useful to the pupils. In the larger schools there is an increasing tendency to employ full time professional librarians. As to the infants' and junior schools, however, most teachers would agree that it is probably best to have small collections actually in the classrooms so that the teacher can make use of books as an essential part of his teaching. These class libraries may with advantage be supplemented by a library room for the school as a whole, and, of course, there should be some central storage for books from which the class collections can be supplemented and exchanged.

Generally, the libraries in the schools are provided not by the public libraries but by the Education Committee. Nevertheless in many cases the Education Committee seeks the cooperation of the Library Committee and especially is this the case in the counties, where all public library work comes under the direction of the County Education Committee. Frequently, however, in towns where library provision and education are quite separate, the public library will be responsible for providing, maintaining and supervising school libraries and will be paid for this work from education funds.

Another service sometimes given by the public library and sometimes given in other ways is the hospital library. I believe that it should be the responsibility of the public library to ensure well stocked, adequately staffed hospital libraries because, after all, the people who are in hospital are ordinary public library patrons when they are well enough to be at home. In practice, library service is given in three different ways. Some few hospitals maintain their own independent libraries staffed by qualified professional librarians who may be helped by volunteers. Others get help from the local public library which supplies books and some staff help. The majority get books from the British Red Cross, the actual work of delivery being done mostly by volunteers.

Nearly all technical colleges and schools of art and of commerce now have their own libraries, which are, to an increasing extent, in charge of qualified professional librarians. Though primarily intended for the use of students and staff a few, in the county areas, are extending their work and helping local industrial concerns in need of technical information.

Those in need of more highly specialized scientific and technical information are served in several ways. Many industrial and commercial organizations maintain their own library and information services. These are supplemented by the libraries of various research departments, such as the Fuel Research Station, Launderers' Research Association, Non-Ferrous Metals Research Association and so on, and by the great national scientific libraries—those of the Patent Office and the Science Museum. The former is shortly to be expanded into a national reference library of science and technology and the work of building up a national lending library in the same fields has already begun. It is housed in Yorkshire and embraces a comprehensive collection of periodicals in all languages, of which both originals and photo copies are available for loan. All the various government departments, as well as the Houses of Parliament, have their own libraries, most of which will admit, on request, the serious enquirer and some of them lend to approved borrowers.

There is also an immense variety of other specialized collections provided by professional and other societies and organizations with all kinds of special interests. Those engaged in the professions of medicine and the law are very well provided for. There are in Great Britain many libraries, great and small, general and highly special, established to make books and other sources of information readily available to all, and, as in every country, these special, university and national libraries are steadily being established and expanded. It is important, I feel, to show how they are gradually working more and more closely together for the general good.

When I started work nearly fifty years ago, everyone who came into the library in which I was a very junior assistant could obtain only those books which we ourselves possessed. This library was probably better than most but we had very little money. Therefore many readers had to go away disappointed—and even more people never came near us because they didn't dream we would be able to help them. Today it is true to say that the reader who goes to his local library, whether it is a tiny village centre in the loneliest part of the country or a large central city library, and no matter now specialized and unusual the book he seeks, will be almost certain to get it. To give an example, of the people who ask at my own library for something I haven't got or can't buy, less than two in a hundred do not eventually get what they want. The same is true of most other public libraries. And it is equally true that the librarians of non-public specializing libraries frequently turn to the cooperative system and borrow both from other special libraries and from public libraries. This service has been made possible by the development of cooperation between libraries of all kinds. And, before I describe our system, let me make this, to my mind, very important observation. Cooperation helps libraries of all kinds and all sizes. We used to think that it would result in the smallest and worst libraries getting a lot of material that they should buy for themselves at the expense of the larger and better libraries—and, of course, it must be agreed that some libraries often do borrow books they should buy. But, on the whole it is the biggest and best libraries that borrow—and also lend—the most. Why? Because their ability to serve the more specialized reader has attracted to the library readers who had never before found it worth while to use them— as well as to give a wider, more specialized supply to existing borrowers.

This tempts me to digress and, before continuing my sketch of our

PLATE I

The Reference Room of the Lamont Library at Harvard, the first library building to be planned primarily to serve the undergraduate students of a major university. The object is to bring together in one place the books, periodicals, recordings, etc., which are necessary to pursue studies in course, afford opportunity to read for personal enjoyment, and form a broad acquaintance with the total intellectual inheritance. The library opened with some 40,000 titles and, being in the shadow of Widener, one of the ranking research libraries of the world, will probably be kept to 100,000 or less. Steps were taken not merely to remove barriers between books and readers but to create in the same act a facility with as many built-in aids to good work as possible.

Chapter 2

PLATE 2

Elementary School Library, New York City. Conceived as a center for materials of various kinds which have demonstrated their value as aids to instruction, the library includes books, films, film strips, graphic illustrations, maps, pictures and other audiovisual aids such as models, mounted specimens, etc. This picture was taken while a class in elementary science was in session. All of the school libraries and librarians under the New York Board of Education are under the supervision of a central Bureau of Libraries, which is directed by an experienced, professionally trained librarian.

Chapter 2

PLATE 3

Library staff of Dunn and Bradstreet, Inc., New York. An example of library service to
business. The function of Dunn and Bradstreet is to furnish business men with the information necessary to make sound credit, sales and management decisions. The business
library staff supports this function by making published data readily available to
company personnel. It also provides an extension of company services by its reference
service to credit report subscribers and to the business public.

Front, l. to r.: Librarian (standing) and secretary, reference assistant, cataloging
assistant, clerk (at mail desk), order assistant; back, l. to r.: assistant librarian,
reference librarian, catalog librarian. The library has a collection of 16,000 volumes,
17,000 pamphlets, and 215 vertical-file drawers.

Chapter 2

PLATE 4

"Popular libraries" have been described as "collections of light reading for people who
read little and study less".

By contrast, this reading room in the New York Public Library is filled with serious
readers, and the building which houses the room, along with others, has been described
as "essentially a community of scholars"—although the preponderance of inquirers
are not scholars by profession. With its eighty circulating branches and its central
Reference Department, the New York Public Library, while not altogether typical,
illustrates the policy of the modern public library of providing, in cooperation with
neighbouring libraries, a balanced program of library service for the community as
a whole—for those who work with their minds and those who enjoy the things of the
mind.

Chapter 2

PLATE 5

The success of the library hinges on the qualifications of the librarian. Here is an example of a library which succeeds in spite of limited funds for books (note the small collection) and limited physical accommodations because of the imaginative efforts of a librarian who is a specialist in children's library work.

Chapter 4

PLATE 6

Information Desk of the New York Public Library. Located at the center of a metropolitan community, the experience of this Library vividly illustrates the scale on which
library materials must be collected, organized and made available with the aid of a
trained staff in order to meet the information and research requirements of modern
scholarship, modern business and modern government. Information experts at this
Desk answer—by telephone, by mail, and by personal query—some 3,000 questions a
day. The Desk itself is an "island" in the Public Catalog Room where 10,000,000
cards list most of the Reference Department's 4,000,000 books.

Chapter 4

PLATE 7

Main Reading Room of the Library of Congress. Established by and for Congress in 1800, the Library now serves other government agencies as well as the general public and heads up services to libraries which are used throughout the United States and in many libraries elsewhere. The main building was erected in 1897, an annex in 1939. The collection is made up of 12,000,000 books and enough maps, manuscripts, musical scores, etc., to bring the total number of items to more than 39,000,000. The work of the Library requires a staff of over 2700, a budget of $14,000,000 a year and several acres (3.5) of floor space.

Chapter 4

PLATE 8

The headquarters staff of the American Library Association. For many years, while the Association's leadership role was being defined, its activities were handled by elected officers without pay; but as the program and membership expanded, a full-time staff became a necessity. This picture was taken in December, 1961, in front of the new headquarters building when final preparations were being made for it to be occupied. Seated in the front row, center, is David H. Clift, Executive Director of the Association.

Chapter 4

PLATE 9

The American Library Association meeting in General Session in 1961. Organized in 1876 by a small band of librarians, the Association now has a membership of 25,000. In the United States are several national library associations, each with its special responsibilities, but the ALA is the only one that includes librarians from libraries of all types. It takes the lead in activities which affect the entire library profession. Strong surges of opinion have now and again threatened to splinter library leadership into factions representing libraries of major types, but each time the judgment that the library movement will benefit most by pursuing specialized interests within the framework of an organization representing the profession as a whole has prevailed.

Chapter 4

Growing recognition of the public library as the foundation of a national library system is related to the contribution it makes to child development. No aspect of public library service has been more successful than service to children—and none is received with greater enthusiasm.

Chapter 5

This High School Library in New York City shows necessary adjustments in program to students whose work is becoming more advanced. The picture was taken during a period of instruction in the use of periodical indexes and other works of reference, a knowledge of which will facilitate intellectual effort not only in high school but in still higher studies—and indeed throughout life. The setting is a well-lighted room, with limited seating, which has been made inviting by attractive books, careful use of displays, bulletin boards and low, free-standing bookcases. Student assistants in the background join in handling routine work of the library.

Chapter 5

PLATE 12

When a student first ventures to use a well-equipped research library, he is handicapped by lack of familiarity with the complex bibliographical apparatus which is available to aid him. The Reference Department of the Columbia University Libraries, in charge of Constance M. Winchell (at the far end of the table), regularly offers instruction in the use of the library to groups when the service is requested by a Professor. To the right is a small section of the main reference collection, which has helped form the Winchell *Guide to Reference Books* while being shaped by it. Behind the class is a file of proof sheets of Library of Congress catalog cards. It is maintained as a means of bringing the printed National Union Catalog up to date. Elsewhere in the room is the main catalog, an alphabetical file of 4,000,000 cards. It enables a reader to locate by author, title or subject any work in any of the Columbia libraries.

Chapter 5

PLATE 13

Commencement Day at Columbia University when relatives and friends of candidates
for degrees gather to watch the traditional ceremony of graduation in front of Butler
Library, in the background. This building houses practically all of the library resources
belonging to the University in the humanities and social sciences except law, journal-
ism, fine arts, music, architecture, and literature in the East Asiatic languages. It houses
on the fifth and sixth floors the graduate School of Library Service with an enrollment
of over 350 students. The Columbia statutes vest administrative responsibility for all
library materials belonging to the University in a Director of Libraries. The offices of
the Director and other central offices of administration are here also.

Chapter 5

PLATE 14

The library system of Columbia University and affiliated institutions. The campus is dominated by *two* library buildings: Butler Library (1), which has served as head-quarters of the system since the building was erected in 1934; and monumental Low Memorial Library (2) erected in 1897, now used partly as a library, partly for University offices. For convenience, libraries belonging to the Columbia corporation are set up in 10 other buildings, 8 of which are marked in the aerial view of the campus above (3). The libraries serving separate corporations closely affiliated with Columbia include: Barnard College (4), Teachers College (5) and Union Theological Seminary (6). All of these libraries cooperate both to economize on expenditures and to combine their resources in serving readers. Three libraries (law, engineering and the Barnard College library) are being transferred to new buildings not shown in this picture. Floor space for library purposes at Columbia amounts to one square foot out of every five for the University as a whole.

Chapter 5

PLATE 15

Exterior of the Holborn Central Library. Structure is of reinforced concrete. Partitions are flexible. Electrical heating equipment is embedded in the floors. A library highly praised not only for utilizing advanced features of library construction but for the skill shown in overcoming physical and legal limitations and producing a building so well adapted to the purposes it serves.

Chapter 7

PLATE 16

On entering the new Holborn Central Library, the reader is taken at once into the lending library, shown above, where he is surrounded by 45,000 well-selected books of pleasing appearance, all on open shelves. The desk of the Reader's Adviser stands in the centre, the public catalog to the left. A stack room is directly below. Also on the lower ground floor: a periodicals reading room, a children's library and theatre (entered by separate stairway inside main entrance).

Chapter 7

PLATE 17

A view of the first floor showing the Reference Library of 10,000 volumes. The Library is furnished with individual study tables, a microfilm reader and a photocopying machine. On the same floor: a commerce library, local history collection and study carrels. Second floor: stacks for 25,000 volumes, gramophone record library, bindery, administrative offices, work rooms and staff accommodations. Top floor: a lecture hall with 250 seats, space for exhibitions and picture-lending service.

Chapter 7

PLATE 18

Part of the Music and Drama Library located on the first floor of the Plymouth Central Library. The City Librarian found, in one check on use, that over 2700 citizens of Plymouth were borrowing music or plays from this room for the purpose of giving public performances. This room stands near the Reference Library of 20,000 volumes, a local history collection of 20,000 items and, on the ground floor below, an open-access lending library and a children's library.

Chapter 7

PLATE 19

A Branch of Buckinghamshire County Library showing street-level accessibility,
modern display practices used to stimulate reading interests, all in a garden-like
setting where one approaches a home for good reading, not a chilly institution devoid
of pleasant associations.

Chapter 7

PLATE 20

Inside the Beaconsfield Branch Library. An example of planning which unites grace of line, cheerful colour and convenient physical arrangements. The Library serves all the community, from the veteran reader to the child who first enters the door to the great world of books.

Chapter 7

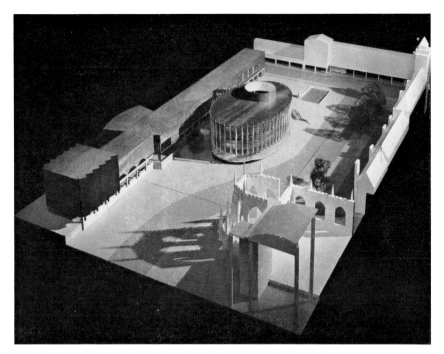

PLATE 21

A model showing the proposed elliptically shaped central library for lending and reference at Coventry, 180 feet long and 60 feet high. Narrow vertical windows stretch from the ground to the flat roof. The pointed polished aluminium mullions extend about two feet above the roof parapet. Access from inside to different parts of the building is afforded by a ramp which spirals round an open well, lit by a circular roof light visible in the picture. Glimpses of the old and new Cathedrals are in the bottom right hand corner.

Chapter 7

PLATE 22

The British Museum's transformation from a museum of treasures and relics to a great centre for scholarly work in the humanities was one of the historic steps in the evolution of the modern research library. The stately reading room shown above was opened in 1857. To it came students and scholars from all over the world but especially from the younger English-speaking countries. They were attracted by uncommonly rich collections of printed books and manuscripts, by catalogues which pioneered modern methods of bibliographical access, and by a stimulating intellectual climate. Panizzi, Proctor, Pollard, Garnett, Fortescue are among the long line of librarians and bibliographers who united to define a new course for the Museum and add lustre to its reputation. The day of the library of record passed with the nineteenth century, but perhaps no library upheld this ideal longer than the Museum. The cosmopolitan character of its collections is illustrated by the fact not only that they were strong in all major languages, but that most readers found them at least the equal of the best collections in their homeland.

Chapter 8

PLATE 23

New Library of the University of Sheffield. The façade of the 155-foot square main floor at the top features a wall of glass, broken into 28 vertical planes. Located on this floor are: an imposing reading room for 256 readers, a reading room stack, periodicals reading room where some 1500 current journals are accommodated, a postgraduate reading room with carrels for microfilm reading, library work space, and a spacious area near the stairs to take care of circulation activities, the card catalogue, printed bibliographies and other heavily used works of reference. Turnstiles and control counter are located at the landing on the mezzanine floor on the way down. Nearby are the Librarian's office and an exhibition hall about 80 × 20 feet. Service facilities on the ground floor include cloak rooms, photographic rooms and service elevator near the loading dock. Directly below the reading room are four stack levels with space for about 850,000 volumes.

Chapter 8

PLATE 24

The Information desk of Central Reference in the Edinburgh Public Library.
Recorded use of the half million volumes in the library exceeds 5,000,000 a year.
Reading is heavy in the humanities as in other fields, but requests for information fall
most heavily in science, technology and the social sciences.

Chapter 8

PLATE 25

National Central Library, London. The apex of one of the most carefully perfected systems of interlibrary cooperation in the world. Ten regions comprising numerous cooperating libraries of various types each seek to meet readers' requests from their own resources. The National Central Library serves as a clearing-house for locating in other regions, or in its own collection, books needed for serious work which are not available in the region where the request originates. Bibliographical facilities of the Library include a union catalogue with more than 2,000,000 entries. Resources of co-operating libraries total not less than 20,000,000 books and many thousands of sets of periodicals. Other activities include serving as a national centre for information about books and aiding in the allocation of duplicates to suitable British and overseas libraries.

Chapter 8

PLATE 26

The Library of the University of Heidelberg. Chartered in 1385, this is the oldest university in the German realm. No mediaeval university rose to eminence more rapidly, and in the nineteenth century it was in the vanguard of the movement which gave the university rank as one of the leading institutions of civilized man. Among the numerous factors which account for the origin of universities in Western Europe, and their gradual spread to other parts of the world, was the gradual accumulation over centuries of a recorded social inheritance, custodianship for which it took centuries to arrange. Today the intellectual record is entrusted to libraries. The emergence of the modern university, as distinguished from its progenitor of mediaeval times, is closely associated with discovery of the relation of library resources and services to the advancement of learning. The German universities led the way in acting upon this insight.

Chapter 10

PLATE 27

A section of the reading room of the University of Bonn where current periodicals are conveniently displayed in a setting with homelike accommodation for readers.

Chapter 10

PLATE 28

Düsseldorf Public Library. Ground floor of 460 square metres, with sandstone exterior.
A vertical plane of slate interrupts the general theme of glass and metal. Over the
entrance, a sculpture of two readers.

Chapter 11

PLATE 29

The Children's Room. A collection of about 6000 books for readers up to the age of 14. Attractiveness is heightened by the use of cheerful, unobtrusive colours and fabrics. Floor space is divided by a graceful landing, which makes it possible to use the room for simple dramatic productions.

Chapter 11

PLATE 30

Interior of the ground floor from the East. Two levels of a circulation room for adults are connected with a stairway having a web-like transparency which leaves the view of the room from any angle unbroken. Book shelves are a combination of steel and wood. Readers are aided in finding their way among book sections by subjects printed on strips of lucite.

Chapter 11

PLATE 31

The same room from the West. To the left is the charging desk and, farther on, the union catalogue. This catalogue is arranged alphabetically but the library provides a subject catalogue also. It stands opposite the windows in the gallery.

Chapter 11

PLATE 32

The Reading Room. To the right and across the end of the room are displayed 100 to 150 periodicals, but the collection consists mainly of some 2000 handbooks and reference works, to the left. Dailies are in an adjoining room, directly behind the viewer.

Chapter 11

PLATE 33

The Music Library. Subject literature is on open shelves in front and to the right. Scores are behind the desk to the left.

Chapter 11

PLATE 34

Auditorium. For literary and musical events. Planned for not more than 80 persons.
A room of simplicity and dignity, with gentle colours in which blues and greys pre-
dominate.

Chapter 11

PLATE 35

Children with picture books in the Children's Department of Hørsholm Public Library,
a very characteristic Danish library building.

Chapter 13

PLATE 36

Men at sea. The Public Libraries Act extends library service to those sections of the community which are prevented from normal use of public libraries. For example the state grants a subsidy to the Seafarers' Library, which provides collections of books for the merchant and royal navies. The seamen above have borrowed their books from the ship's library. This library is another link with home. It is a source of pleasure during hours off and helps live minds to stay in touch with the world that lies beyond the deck and hold.

Chapter 13

PLATE 37

Men doing their national service. Local libraries in cooperation with the Armed Forces
Welfare Service provide library service for soldiers. These are consulting an open-shelf
collection of books and magazines which is housed in one of their barracks.

Chapter 13

PLATE 38

Cooperation between school and public library. The Primary Education Act allows
large subsidies for the establishment of school libraries in new schools being built. This
has had particular importance in country districts and many excellent premises have
been acquired which combine the functions of school library and public library.
Example of a combination of these functions in a rural district, showing desks, books
on open shelves, displays to stimulate reading interest and frequently used reference
works.

Chapter 13

PLATE 39

Responsibility for the development of public library service in Denmark is centralized in a government department entitled The State Inspectorate for Public Libraries. Erik Allersleve Jensen, a public librarian of broad experience, is the Director.

Chapter 13

PLATE 40

Cooperative library binding. The Danish Bibliographical Office arrange for central-ized binding of public library books. A view which shows this work in progress.

Chapter 13

PLATE 41

Book-boat. Svendborg County Library is serving a district of many small islands which can only be visited by sea. While Denmark makes liberal use of bookmobiles, in other regions, this district is served by a book-boat. Islanders are shown looking for books during one of its visits.

Chapter 13

Newton Associates

PLATE 42

The Canadian Library Association began with cramped quarters, limited funds and a strong sense of purpose. In this headquarters scene of 1954, note the makeshift collating bins of galvanized iron, the closely huddled desks, the necessity of using space where the Association's typing was carried on to store posters and publications kept in stock for sale.

Library associations take form in the minds of men and women who are dedicated to their work, and the point is so graphically illustrated by Canadian experience that more than one date can be used to mark the beginning of the Association. It has existed on paper since 1901. In the 1940's, after careful analysis of reasons for failure to get started, it was decided to begin in a very simple fashion with a voluntary committee representing the provinces and different types of libraries, with one full-time librarian, a small clerical staff and complementary quarters. As experimentation with national projects succeeded and librarians were further unified through field trips of the Secretary, the time came to form a permanent membership organization in 1946. Each year the work is surveyed to see where failures have occurred and where improvements can be made in the future. A prominent factor in the success of the Association has been the capacity of leading librarians to face hardships cheerfully and to work together in unison.

Chapter 14

PLATE 43

Photograph of model of the National Library of Canada. The building is located near the Ottawa River and the background shows the Hills of Quebec. The structure to the side of the building is the auditorium which will seat 250 persons. This is the view of the building from the side.

Chapter 14

National Film Board

PLATE 44

Canadians have helped blaze the trail in extending library service to people in thinly populated areas. One of the historic experiments was the Fraser Valley Regional Library, the first regional library to be organized in Canada. The photograph shows a book truck which carries a widely varied stock of books. Note the interest of the teenagers. The truck stops at specific times on its journey through the Valley.

Chapter 14

National Film Board

PLATE 45

The Lester Blackmore Memorial Library, Clarenville, Trinity North, Newfoundland, is part of a regional system which covers the entire province. Because of the fiords of this island, the library is organized in many small coordinated regional groups—the whole supervised by the Central Provincial Agency in the Provincial capital.

Chapter 14

PLATE 46

This scene in a private home shows the family hanging the work of art which has been
borrowed from the lending library of Canadian art of the London Public Library &
Art Museum. Note the carrying bag in which the picture was taken home to the right
of the photograph.

Chapter 14

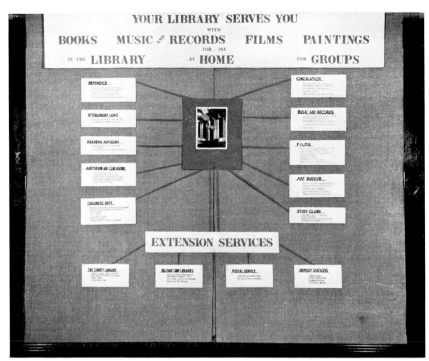

PLATE 47

The London, Ontario, Public Library poster board outlines the services given to its community.

Chapter 14

PLATE 48

North Central Regional Library of Saskatchewan. Miss Gracie Campbell the chief librarian (in flowered dress), is introduced to a local councillor by Miss Marion Gilroy, chief of Regional Services for the province of Saskatchewan. The councillor is considering establishing a unit of the regional library in his village, and after discussing the matter with Miss Gilroy, has come to see the Regional Library in action at its headquarters in Prince Albert. This photograph became part of a film entitled "Books for Beaver River" produced by the National Film Board of Canada. Miss Gilroy has recently made a survey of the Canadian Arctic for regional service at the request of the Department of Northern Affairs and National Resources and is currently surveying the Lakeshore towns on the St. Lawrence in the vicinity of Montreal for the Province of Quebec.

Chapter 14

Mail Star Chronicle Herald, Halifax

PLATE 49

An example of a project of national importance undertaken by the Canadian Library Association was the filming of newspaper files of historic interest. Recorded here is a moment of triumph—completion of the filming of the first newspaper in Canada, *The Halifax Herald*. It took some fifteen years to collect the files, borrowed from more than a dozen institutions in Canada, the United States and abroad. From left to right: Mrs. Herman Nyland, CLA Councillor, Halifax; Miss Elizabeth Morton, Executive Director of the Association, and Miss Ruby Wallace, President-elect of the Association, Sydney, Nova Scotia.

Chapter 14

PLATE 50

The first temporary quarters of the National Library of Canada were in the Public Archives Building. Here the Union Catalog of the libraries of Canada began its compilation. In this photograph is to be seen the catalog cards being photographed on a Recordak Machine.

Chapter 14

PLATE 51

This photograph shows the roll of prints of the catalog cards photographed in the previous picture. The roll is stamped by the first clerk with the name of the library photographed. The second clerk cuts the cards, which now measure $3'' \times 5''$, and the third clerk files them into the catalog. The background shows the files of the Union Catalog when this project was located in the Public Archives.

Chapter 14

PLATE 52

The regional libraries of British Columbia give service to the schools and this photograph is typical of a library hour.

Chapter 14

system of cooperation, to tell you what is my own philosophy of book provision by public libraries—a philosophy shared, I believe, by many of my colleagues. It is this: The public library—with the help of other libraries—should seek to offer the maximum opportunity to those who need books. We must, of course, keep in mind our responsibilities towards all kinds of readers, young and old, and try with our limited resources both to give the maximum benefit and to secure the maximum use of all our materials. But we want to be as sure as we can that everyone who genuinely, seriously, for any purpose important to him, seeks a particular book, no matter how "individual", specialized or difficult to obtain, shall get it somehow. We achieve this in two ways: by giving preference in our own purchasing to books of individual significance and importance at the expense of more trivial and ordinary books that can be bought at little cost by those who want them; and by making our utmost contribution to schemes of cooperation which I shall now describe—though before I do so I must say most emphatically that inter-loan schemes must never lead to neglect of local provision. Each local public library must have always on its own shelves a sufficient, representative, up-to-date stock to meet all but the most specialized needs of the public. This is important for two main reasons. One is that an open access library is a great educational force. It can not only meet the existing needs of readers; it can show them, through the books on its open shelves, much of the wealth of material available, of the richness of life and experience; it can open doors leading to new worlds and teach them how books make them happier, more effective, more con-tented, giving them a better understanding of themselves and of their fellow men throughout the world. The other reason is that it is clearly very much less expensive of money and time for readers to get what they want when they want it from their own library. Borrowing from other libraries is expensive, of staff time, postal costs and so on. And the impor-tance of having material on their own shelves available immediately is possibly even greater in the case of the specialist library.

To return to our schemes for cooperation, however: the organization for the inter-loan of books and periodicals is a simple one. England is divided into nine regions, in each of which there is a regional bureau. With one exception, there is at each bureau a union catalogue of books in stock at the various libraries in the region. When any library requires, for one of its readers, a particular item which is not in that library's own stock and which it cannot or does not wish to buy for itself, it sends an application to the regional bureau. I said "cannot" obtain because, of course a high proportion of the books required are older, out of print, works of which it may be difficult to buy even second-hand copies. If any library in the region has a copy—and often there are several copies

F

available—that library is asked to send it by post to the library at which it is wanted. If, however, there is no copy available within the region, the regional bureau at once sends the request to the National Central Library which is in London.

The National Central Library was founded, as the Central Library of Studies, in 1916, with substantial financial help for several years from the Carnegie United Kingdom Trust. Now it is supported by the National Government, from which it gets over 80 per cent of its funds, and by contributions from many of the libraries which use it. At the National Central Library is an extensive union catalogue built up from information received from the Regional Bureaux and also from the non-public libraries, some 300 in number, which take part in the scheme. These include the libraries of universities and colleges and of a great variety of specialized libraries interested in different aspects of science, technology, history, the fine arts, and so on.

If the required item appears in this union catalogue the library with a copy is, as before, asked to send it where it is needed. If there is no copy shown in this catalogue, one of several things may happen. For example, the staff may ask an appropriate specialist library if it has the book and, if not, whether it is willing to acquire and lend it. Again, lists of required items are circulated at frequent intervals to the other Regional Bureaux and to suitable libraries. Apart from this process the National Central Library itself has a collection of books built up over the years with particular regard to those kinds of books which experience has shown to be not readily available or not to be borrowed from the local reference libraries. The required item may be found in this stock or may be purchased for it if possible. Finally, if the book is one published abroad, application may be made to the appropriate centre in that country.

As a result of this system a high proportion of the required items are ultimately provided. I stress ultimately because, though many books can be provided in two or three days, it takes several days and occasionally even weeks to trace and despatch others. Delay usually happens because a library asked to supply a book has already lent it to one of its own readers, when either the applicant has to wait for it to be returned or, if there are other libraries with copies, for the application to be sent on. So experiments are now being made with Telex and Teleprinter which will cut down the time involved, as enquiry can be made at several libraries in succession or simultaneously. What matters, however, is that already the individual student no longer has to rely solely upon the resources of his own library. He can draw upon the resources of a great many and varied libraries and thus has several millions of volumes ultimately at his disposal. There are also similar central libraries in Scotland and Ireland. In Scotland the cost is shared equally between the national government and the cooperating libraries.

The next step in co-operation was to try and strengthen the total resources of the cooperating libraries. Every library is, naturally, most concerned with the needs of its own readers. This is especially true of the public libraries which therefore tend to buy much the same books, since they have to meet much the same kinds of demands. What was needed was a plan to make sure that *every* book was bought by at least one library in each region and so, through the inter-lending scheme just described, was available everywhere. The first such scheme was begun by the London public libraries a few years ago, and now there are similar schemes operating in other regions. The whole field of knowledge is divided between the cooperating libraries, each of which undertakes to buy on publication every British book dealing with its own section. For convenience each library has allotted to it certain parts of the Dewey Decimal schedules. My own library, for example, is responsible for books on the fine arts, including music, as well as for certain other subjects. It must be understood, of course, that every library still buys all the books in *all* fields that it needs for its own readers and to ensure them a wide comprehensive selection. Thus most worthwhile books are bought for all libraries. What the scheme ensures is that at the very least *one* library will buy everything as it is published, no matter how specialized. And the scheme goes further in two important respects. Firstly, each library tends to buy older material so as to make its own special collections as good as possible. Secondly, each library makes itself responsible for keeping at least one copy of every available book in its own subject field. As most libraries have very limited storage accommodation what happened formerly was that libraries used to throw away the less used books in order to make room for those more likely to be needed. As a consequence, every library tended to keep the same books and to throw away the same books, so that in time no library had any copy of certain books. Now, before we throw away anything not belonging to our own special field, we offer it to the library to whose field it does belong and, if it does not already possess a copy, that library accepts and keeps our copy. In this way we can be sure that somewhere in London we can obtain any book that was ever in stock at any London public library. This scheme was later extended to cover novels and children's books. So far the libraries taking part in these specialization schemes, which are, let it be remembered, entirely voluntary, have only been *required* to buy and keep books in English but already many are voluntarily extending their collection to include important works in other languages.

It is appropriate to mention here another example of cooperation.

Surely among the first books in foreign languages to be made available are outstanding works of literature—novels, poems, plays and the like. Consequently the London metropolitan libraries some years ago devised a plan to ensure that somewhere in London there should be representative, if small, collections in such languages as Hungarian, Polish, Yiddish, Swedish, and Rumanian. Though public demand may be small it could nevertheless be met by this cooperation.

As I have already noted a great many non-public libraries already take part in the work of the National Central Library and the regional bureaux. Two other types of cooperation are developing which are still further linking them together so that resources and opportunities may be improved. Firstly, there are several schemes which unite libraries of all kinds which are specially interested in the same field, for example, those concerned with aeronautics, electronics, fuel and power, furniture and textiles. The librarians in each such group meet to consult regarding the provision of expensive books and periodicals, seeking, by avoiding unnecessary duplication and by mutual assistance, to ensure that each can make the maximum contribution to the total resources available to all. Secondly, there are schemes which unite all the different kinds of library in a district—public, university, research, including the libraries of industrial concerns and professional organizations. The first of these local schemes was started for the Sheffield area several years ago. Another excellent example operates in the north west of Greater London, where libraries of many different types and sizes share their resources of books, periodicals and expert staffing, maintaining central catalogues of periodicals, abstracts and bibliographies and a central bureau at which enquiries of all kinds can be handled. Ten public library systems and over 70 industrial and other firms and organizations, ranging from the very large such as Kodak and the General Electric Co. to the very small, take part in the scheme.

Since 1952 full and accurate information about new British publications has been given in the British National Bibliography, published weekly and cumulated at regular intervals with annual volumes and five yearly indexes. Printed catalogue cards are also now available at a very low cost. Here is another valuable cooperative project which, in addition to its primary purpose of giving information, can be used to reduce substantially the work of cataloguing and classifying which, formerly, every library had to do for its own needs. Entries are classified by the Dewey Decimal system which is used by the great majority of public and many special libraries, though several others use the U.D.C. or the Bliss systems, a few the Library of Congress classification, and some have devised special schemes to meet their own requirements. So far as public libraries are concerned there is a great deal to be said for adopting a widely used scheme. On the one hand, it is of great help to the users to find the same arrangement of shelves and catalogues in each library they may use. On the other hand, a great part of the labour of providing catalogues can be avoided if standard printed cards are used.

Most libraries in Great Britain provide card catalogues, though a few use sheafs and a few issue printed catalogues. Many years ago—before the card catalogue was introduced—most libraries issued their own printed catalogues but these gave way to cards because the printed catalogue quickly became out of date as new books were bought and old ones withdrawn from stock. But those who have restarted to print point out that cooperative schemes for book preservation mean that even if the library with the printed catalogue has long thrown away its own copy, it can readily borrow it from somewhere else. And it cannot be denied that a printed catalogue is very much pleasanter, quicker and easier to consult than one on cards.

I have spoken so far mostly about the book stock of libraries but I would like to devote the rest of my limited time to three other aspects of library provision. Firstly, I attach great importance to offering users the maximum possible facilities so that full use of the library may be as easy, as convenient and as pleasant as possible. I have already stressed the vital importance of open access to the shelves which is needed to the maximum possible extent in all kinds of library, not only in the public library. Even if space is limited, open access under crowded conditions is better than no access at all, but with proper support for the library such conditions should not be necessary, and buildings should be roomy, attractive and well kept. Unfortunately, many additional branch librar- ies are needed in Great Britain and many of the older central libraries have long become unsuitable and too small. The greatest expansion in holdings has taken place since the war, and until recently there have been restrictions of building, imposed by the Government, which have prevented adequate increases and improvements in library buildings.

As it is very important that libraries should remain open as long as sufficient readers are likely to use them, I am glad to say that all public central and full time branch libraries remain open every weekday for nine to ten hours, for example from ten in the morning to eight at night. A majority of special libraries are, of course, required, and therefore open, only during normal working hours, but there is a tendency for some of the more important ones, such as our national library, the British Museum, to offer increased hours in the evening.

Though attractive premises, up-to-date methods, pleasant conditions and generous facilities are desirable the most important factors are book stocks and staffing. Probably the latter is the more important, as without good staff the best stocks will not be fully exploited, while good staff can make the most of limited stocks. The importance of appropriate professional education for the staff of libraries of all types has been increasingly recognized since the Library Association introduced the first examinations nearly sixty years ago. Today it can be said that all seeking professional posts on the staffs of public and government libraries and most of those professionally employed in special libraries and universities must have become chartered librarians. A "chartered librarian" is one who, having undergone an appropriate course of professional education and worked for a minimum of three years in an approved library, has passed the Registration Examination or the Final Examination of the Library Association. These persons are entered on the Library Association's register in two categories—those who have passed the Registration Examination and satisfied other requirements are registered as Associates; more senior librarians, who have at least five years practical experience and who have passed the Final Examination, may become Fellows.

With the exception of London University, which has our only University School of Librarianship, the Library Association is the only body holding examinations in this field, and the syllabus is at present under revision. At present, however, it consists of three parts—the first a "first professional examination", for non-graduates, which is designed to assess the candidate's suitability for library work. The second, the Registration Examination, is of intermediate standard and is a suitable qualification for the junior professional assistants and "assesses the candidate's possession of the knowledge necessary to competent practising librarians", whereas the Final is the appropriate examination for the senior librarians. The Registration Examination includes papers on classification, cataloguing, bibliography and assistance to readers, library organization and administration and either the history of English literature or the literature of science and technology or the literature of social and political ideas. In the more advanced Final Examination, in addition to certain general papers there are ample alternatives for those working in public, or university, or special libraries and for those especially interested in a field of knowledge, e.g. social sciences, science and technology, medicine, fine arts, music, etc., with a further choice of papers on special aspects of library work, such as archives and work with children.

Preparation for the examinations can be made either by attending a year's full time course at a school of librarianship, or by going to the evening classes available at a great many schools. The full time course is much to be preferred, as it enables the student to devote his whole energy to study and brings him into close contact with his teachers and fellow students. There are nine colleges offering whole time courses;

only one of these, however, the oldest, established in 1919, is at a university. Most students obtain grants from their local education committee to cover, if necessary, the tuition fees and maintenance. Some schools offer tuition, and consequently some students take courses, for both the Registration and the Final Examinations.

Last year no fewer than 326 new Associates were admitted to the Register. There are today, employed in libraries of all kinds, 3745 Associates and 1628 Fellows. These numbers are not anything like sufficient. For example, if the standards of public library staffing recommended in the Report to the Minister of Education were to be adopted, over 6000 professional librarians would be needed, whereas today only 3206 are so employed. The shortage of qualified staff is due largely to the great development, since the war, of libraries of all kinds, and especially of libraries of industry, scientific research, the government departments and of higher education. Many of these have attracted young men and women from the public library service where, in general, salaries and prospects are at present less attractive. The need for better salaries and opportunities is receiving very serious attention, as indeed it must if suitable recruits are to enter the growing and increasingly important profession of librarianship.

Lastly I must refer to the vital part that has been played by the Library Association. Founded in 1877, its first main purpose was that of encouraging the establishment of public libraries, but the scope of its functions has gradually widened. Though its main function is still to promote the development and improvement of libraries of all kinds, and though it still brings together practising librarians and lay members of library committees and others interested in the improvement of libraries, its most important tasks today are probably those of examination and registration and the collection and dissemination of information. By means of its work in the examination, certification and registration of librarians, it has established librarianship in the eyes of the public and of employers as a profession requiring special training, experience and abilities. This has resulted in far higher standards of efficiency, a closer regard for the techniques of library work, and a sense of social purpose on the part of the librarian. And, of course, it has taught the public that good library service can only be given by suitable, experienced, qualified staff, that it is not a job that anyone can do.

The Library Association now has 13,718 members, of whom 11,651 are individuals engaged in library work in Great Britain and 853 are representatives of the committees and others responsible for libraries of all kinds in this country. Those working outside Great Britain can become corresponding members; there are 845 of them, as well as 370 corresponding institutional members all over the world. There are sections of the Association which look after the particular interests and problems of those employed in particular types of library, such as university and research libraries, reference and special libraries and information services and so on; there is also an organization of branches arranging meetings and other activities throughout the country and within easy reach of all members everywhere.

To sum up, I hope I have shown that although in Great Britain we have a wealth of libraries of different kinds, each with its own particular function and body of users, we have steadily striven to bring them and their librarians together to help one another and thus to improve the resources available to everyone. We have sought to create one library service and one library profession while respecting the need for independence and variety. We have taught one another much by sharing our experience and ideas. We have a great deal yet to do but we are undoubtedly making strides forward.

One final point: in the last few years we have learned that just as the different librarians of one country can benefit by mutual help, encouragement and interchange of ideas and ideals, so can the librarians of the various nations of the world. Therefore it is a fine and wonderful thing to see the idea of cooperation, with all its possibilities, spreading steadily throughout the world. Librarians will themselves, by international cooperation, gain immensely. Much more important, they will thereby be able to give more to their own peoples and so help to bring them closer together for mutual aid and understanding.

9. BOOKS AND LIBRARIES IN OUR TIME III:
INTRODUCTION OF THE THIRD LECTURER

PROF. HAMIT DERELI
University of Ankara

WITH the help of some friendly nations, the Faculty of Letters has arranged an International Series of Lectures on Librarianship. I am happy to introduce to you today our third lecturer who will give the fifth lecture in the Series.

"The true university of these days is a collection of books," said Thomas Carlyle, the nineteenth century thinker. This statement, which was true in the nineteenth century, is of even greater importance for us today. We cannot speak of university education or university research unless we have book collections—the collections which are cataloged, classified and offered to the use of researchers according to modern library methods.

The Faculty of Letters is proud of having a library school which teaches the principles of modern librarianship. I wish to acknowledge the services of my distinguished colleagues who have helped to establish and develop our library school. I wish to thank them here today in your presence.

Our lecturer today is Dr. Rudolf Juchhoff, Librarian of Cologne University. Dr. Juchhoff is Professor Emeritus of Books and Library Science at the Faculty of Philosophy, Cologne University. He is at the same time one of the professors of the library school of the same University. Born in 1894, Dr. Juchhoff has as a scholar specialized in Germanic studies and English literature. He was a librarian in Berlin State Library from 1922 to 1945. After this he was employed to prepare a Union Catalog of Manuscripts. Later he became the Chief of Information Service of German Libraries. In 1947 he served as the chief of the Union Catalog for the Nordrhein-Westfalen libraries. In 1954 he was appointed to be the librarian of Cologne University Library and Director of the Library School of the same University. He has to his credit several publications on library science. It is a great honor for me to introduce to you Dr. Juchhoff.

10. THE LIVING TRADITION OF THE UNIVERSITY AND RESEARCH LIBRARIES IN GERMANY

PROF. DR. RUDOLF JUCHHOFF

Bibliothekar-Lehrinstitut des Landes Nordrhein-Westfalen

Federal Republic of Germany

GERMANY can boast a great variety of libraries adapted to the use of all kinds of readers from the academic scholar to the people who go to a popular library to get a novel for home reading. Owing to the fact that Germany, with the exception of some years under Nazi rule, has always been a federal state, a fact to some extent obscured by the dominating influence of one of the member states, Prussia, there has never been a chance of a national library developing, although the Prussian State Library in Berlin, because of its wealth of books and manuscripts and a number of very important central library agencies, e.g. the Prussian union catalogue, fulfilled to some extent the tasks commonly associated with a national library. But making up for this deficiency there is a greater number of very important regional libraries than perhaps in any other European country. These *Staatsbibliotheken* and *Landesbibliotheken*, in most cases early foundations of the German princes of the various kingdoms, dukedoms and principalities, together with the university libraries and the libraries of the Technical Institutes, which are developing to the status of technical universities, are the backbone of the German system of scholarly libraries. In addition, there are the very important libraries of central institutions for the study of special fields of knowledge, such as the Institute of World Economics and International Trade at Kiel, the Central Institute for the History of Art at Munich, The Latin-American Institute at Berlin and a lot of others. It hardly needs saying that the libraries of institutions like these are growing ever more important as centres of documentation in their respective fields. While these libraries, like all other publicly-owned libraries, are open to people who have occasion to use them for serious study, the libraries of the big associations of industry and commerce and other private corporations cater in the first instance, of course, to the needs of their members; but many of them are now readily accessible to people outside their own membership circles, thus forming part of the national library system with all the implications of give and take within the German interlibrary lending system. The same applies to some of the larger administrative libraries of federal and state authorities. And then there is the youngest but vigorous branch of library activity, the fast growing municipal popular libraries (*Volksbüchereien*) that are catering for the general reader, for his need of information and of leisure reading. They are fulfilling a very important task in a modern democratic society, a task outlined in the (provisional) constitution of the German Federal Republic of 1949: Everybody is entitled to free access to all sources of information. The future of these *Volksbüchereien* or *Öffentliche Büchereien* (the latter name being preferred now by many librarians as equivalent to the English term public library) is bright indeed.

The idea of a university, in German minds, is still that of Wilhelm von Humboldt, the spiritual founder of Berlin University (1810). A professor's task is twofold: adding to the sum total of human knowledge by original research (*Forschung*) and training his student (*Lehre*) by transmitting the essential knowledge in his academic field in his lectures and by supervising and discussing the student's own beginner's research. This idea is, of course, reflected in the library of a university or, for that matter, in the library of a technical university. But it must not be overlooked that university libraries are not limited to the use of professors and students of their respective universities, but are for the use of all who are engaged in research or are reading for further education based on scholarly books. The fact that university libraries are at the same time academic and public libraries is at the root of their dominating position within the whole of the German library system. University librarians together with their colleagues of the state libraries of Berlin and Munich have been in the forefront of all library activity during the nineteenth and twentieth centuries. Most schemes of library organization and of library cooperation have been elaborated by librarians of this type. Therefore this survey of German libraries will centre about the university libraries (including those of technical universities) as representing German library work at its best.

University libraries are directly or indirectly state owned. Their staff are state officials whose salaries conform to the various grades of public servant: higher grade, middle grade and lower grade. Some peculiarities of the distribution of work in a library are to be explained only by keeping this graduation in mind.

Usually university libraries have three departments dealing respectively with new books coming in, with cataloguing and classifying books, and with the books being circulated among readers. They are called *Erwerbungsabteilung* (accessions department), *Katalogabteilung* (cataloguing department) and *Benutzungsabteilung* (lending department). There is also the general administration department and secretariat. Of course there are in most libraries some special departments: manuscripts, incunabula, music, records, etc.

Who does the selection of books for the accession department? The answer will strike most non-German librarians as rather unusual. For unlike the procedure in most countries where professional library committees are responsible in the last resort for the selection of books deemed necessary for the various fields of knowledge represented by the various faculties, in Germany the librarians select the books deemed necessary for the university library. This could not be done unless the higher grade librarian were of academic standing, a man or woman fully trained in a definite academic field. Such training is now a condition of being admitted to the profession of higher grade librarian. The aspiring librarian has to follow a full university course in some accepted field up to what is called *Staatsexamen*, i.e. the final examination required and supervised by the state for its future higher grade civil servants. But unlike other professional candidates, future higher grade librarians (and their confrères of the archives) in addition to their *Staatsexamen*, have to write a dissertation, and pass the oral examination for the doctorate. Thus higher grade librarians are doctors of philosophy or law or theology, etc. While the state examination guarantees a certain breadth of academic learning, the dissertation testifies to the librarian's training in original research work. German libraries adhere to the conviction that only he who has done some research work himself will be able to appreciate the requirements of professors and other research workers as regards books and other documentary material and to devise and organize sound methods of supplying and utilizing such material.

At present, university libraries employ from 6 to 12 librarians of this type (let me call them very loosely "doctor librarians") representing the various faculties of their universities. Some time ago the library committee of the *Deutsche Forschungsgemeinschaft* (German Research Association) set up, as the minimum requirements of the average university library, the following table of the branches of knowledge, each to be represented on the staff by a doctor librarian:

1. Generalia, Philosophy, Theology
2. History and Art History
3. Laws and Political Science
4. Medicine
5. Biological Sciences
6. Pure and Applied Sciences
7. Orientalia
8. Slav Languages and Literatures
9. Germanic and English Languages and Literatures
10. Classical and Romance Philology.

Of course this system will work efficiently in future only if the number of doctor librarians keeps pace with the ever expanding sciences and humanities. These librarians are solely responsible for the selection of books for the university library, each one for his special branch of knowledge as *Fachreferent*. Whereas university professors, as experience has shown, are apt to select books according to their actual research needs in a very specialized field, neglecting books that may be of interest to other workers in neighbouring fields, the *Fachreferenten* are supposed to stand for continuity of accessions and to select, without bias, all important publications necessary for present and future research. The *Fachreferent* will make use of all sources of bibliographical information from national to special bibliographies and the bibliographical parts of the specialized periodicals, in order to be able to estimate the scientific importance of a new publication. The idea that only librarians versed in a special branch of science of the humanities are able to serve the needs of professors and students in a world of ever growing specialization is certainly gaining ground in other countries too. But university librarians wholly independent of the teaching staff of their universities is a concept possible only where, as is the case with German universities, every holder of a chair (Professor ordinarius) is at the same time Director of a university institute (Seminar) with a library of its own. Whereas two generations ago the seminar libraries were fairly good collections of reference works, handbooks and texts, they have grown to quite considerable proportions aiming at becoming self-sufficient research libraries in their special fields. But their growth is largely dependent upon the research interest of the director or co-directors. No wonder that in many cases one can trace the scientific interests of the various chair holders in the selection of books, resulting in the fact that some special aspects of the field of knowledge represented by the department have been over-emphasized to the detriment of other aspects that may interest the following generation. The *Fachreferent* is a safeguard against the same trend developing in the growth of the central university library. The two library services taken together guarantee a system of book supply for all needs that may arise within a university.

Thus to get the right idea of the library resources of a German university one must keep in mind that the university library is supplemented by a circle of institutional libraries, usually representing, in large universities, book stocks about the same size as those of the central library. Institutes of classical philology and ancient history or of Germanic phililogy own libraries from 20,000 to 30,000 volumes.

As a rule there is no administrative relation between the institute libraries and the central university library, no means of influencing, for example, the process of cataloguing books in the institute libraries. All attempts of university librarians to get a hand in administering the institute libraries have failed. That does not mean that there are no personal contacts between the *Fachreferent* of the central library and the directors of the institutes representing his own fields of knowledge. There are, on occasion, consultations between them as to whether the institute or the central library is the best place to buy and stock a very expensive book. And then, complaints of university librarians that the institute libraries suffer from inefficient administration by senior students or assistant tutors are likely to be less frequent in future because an ever-increasing number of institute libraries are employing professionally trained librarians of the middle-grade type.

As the output of research literature increases from year to year, not only in bulk but in diversity of languages, the need of linguistic specializ-ation among university librarians is being felt, in other words the need of *Sprachreferenten* as well as *Fachreferenten*. A *Fachreferent* with special knowledge of Near Eastern languages might be assigned the task of keeping abreast of the important literature in these languages and of assisting his colleagues, let us say in law, in selecting the relevant law books on the assumption that a scholar who knows the language, litera-ture, and history of a nation is to a certain degree interested in other cultural activities of the nation as well.

The independence and responsibility of the *Fachreferent* in selecting books are restricted only by the necessity of distributing funds pro-portionately among the various *Fachreferenten* and of meeting special requirements of the accessions department as regards antiquarian pur-chases or other special occasions of acquiring books. This task falls within the responsibility of the head librarian. In some university libraries it has become the custom, founded on experience of many years, to allocate a definite proportion of the annual purchasing fund to the various *Fachreferenten* with the proviso, of course, of revision if the production of literature is increasing or decreasing in the respective branches of learn-ing. Even in the case of financially well provided libraries it is no easy task to get all the books the *Fachreferenten* think necessary for their special departments, because a substantial proportion of funds is committed in advance to annual subscriptions for periodical publications. The latter are, at any rate in the sciences, even more important than books as a means of making known recent research. A university library must subscribe to a great number of periodicals on an international scale. That takes from 45 to 60 per cent of the available funds. To save money on periodicals could never occur to a librarian's mind; so there is always the difficulty of striking a balance between the money spent on periodi-cals and on books. The situation has been made easier for some time past and will continue easier in the foreseeable future through allocations from the Deutsche Forschungsgemeinschaft for buying foreign periodicals of research value. More will be said about this later.

Almost all German university libraries, but not the libraries of the technical universities, are entitled to receive a free copy of all books, pamphlets and periodicals published within a region defined by special copyright law. In this way certain university libraries situated in a region with important publishing firms are receiving the equivalent of a considerable amount of money. In addition all university libraries (including those of technical universities) participate in a mutual exchange of dissertations when they are published under the aegis of the faculties. Most faculties make publication of a thesis in some form a prerequisite to the granting of a doctor's degree. Exchange of dissertations brings in some thousands of items annually.

All in all, university libraries increase their stock of books each year by from 20,000 to 30,000 bibliographical items (including annual volumes of periodicals). This mass of publications finds its way from the accessions department into the cataloguing department, where they are catalogued according to special rules for the description of titles and for inserting them in alphabetical order. The cataloguing department is the domain of the middle-grade staff mentioned above. The rules now followed by most German libraries are those set up at the end of the last century by librarians of the Prussian State Library and are known as the "Prussian instructions". They have played an important part in assimilating the alphabetical catalogues of German libraries, thus facilitating among other things the making of union catalogues. But after two generations of excellent service certain rules seem to call for revision. While the first part of the instructions, dealing with description of the title-page, defining words like author or editor, etc., seems well adapted to future requirements, the second part, dealing with the alphabetical order of a mass of title-cards, seems no longer adequate to the requirements of the influx of books in a great variety of languages of very different linguistic structure. The Prussian rules of word order are based on the concept of grammatical independence. While they are well adapted to languages like German and the Romance languages, the grammatical structure of which is based on the system of Latin grammar, English no longer fits into this system, to say nothing of the non-Indo-European languages. For years individual librarians and cataloguing committees have been busy devising new rules. A radical change seems desirable towards what German librarians are wont to call mechanical order, i.e. taking as title entry the actual title, word for word, omitting the article when it is the first word. It will be easily understood that switching over to new rules of alphabetical order is not lightly contemplated by librarians responsible for big alphabetical catalogues. Only if the international conference on cataloguing, planned for autumn 1961, paves the way for a really international cataloguing code is there a chance of German librarians contemplating a revision of the Prussian code. Corporate authorship was not considered by the compilers of the Prussian rules. So, as a rule, university libraries have not yet made use of it, although there is a growing awareness among librarians that the concept of corporate authorship can no longer be dispensed with.

Most university libraries have one comprehensive alphabetical catalogue containing the titles of all books, pamphlets and periodicals owned by the library. Some have a separate catalogue of dissertations in order to keep the general catalogue within bounds. As most university libraries have more than 300,000 dissertations already in their stacks and many thousands coming in every year, the growth of the alphabetical catalogue is closely related to the increase in the number of dissertations. Opinion differs as to the advisability of a split catalogue. What may be a gain to some is clearly a loss from the point of view of the user, whether student or librarian, because in many cases a title has to be looked up twice. If an alphabetical catalogue is being used—and there is no German university library not being used to full capacity—there is a danger of the catalogue card deteriorating rapidly; though in an age when photographic reproduction processes are being constantly improved and made cheaper, duplicating a catalogue after some time is not out of the question. But there are other reasons for keeping the general catalogue apart as an instrument for administrative purposes to be used only by trained staff members, and establishing a second alphabetical catalogue for the readers' use. You can keep this second catalogue in bounds to some extent for a long time to come by excluding from it unimportant copyright publications and other material of a non-academic nature, thus constituting an *Auswahlkatalog*, i.e. a selective catalogue. But few libraries can afford the staff necessary for the upkeep of such an additional alphabetical catalogue.

German university libraries have no dictionary catalogues combining author and title entries plus subject entries as normally favoured by American libraries. Instead they have a long tradition of classified or, as the German term is, systematic catalogues. Ever since Göttingen University library, about the middle of the eighteenth century, established a systematic catalogue reflecting the classification on the shelves, this sort of catalogue has been imitated especially by libraries in the northern half of Germany. It is supposed to make it easy for the scholar to get an adequate survey of the state of research in his special field, but in relation to other fields of knowledge. Today German librarians are convinced of the usefulness, even the necessity, of a systematic catalogue as the chief subject catalogue. Much of the activity of the higher grade librarian, the *Fachreferent*, consists of work on this catalogue. His academic training for research stands him in good stead in the same way as when selecting books for the acquisitions department. Moreover, he gets for classification the books which he himself has selected. Thus, well acquainted with the scholarly literature in his own field of study, he is the man to give advice to readers on certain subjects. The *Fachreferenten* as a body form an ideal information department.

There is no uniform system of classification in German university libraries. During the nineteenth century quite a lot of them developed systems of their own, only one, that of Otto Hartwig of Halle, having been made public as *Schema des Realkatalogs der Universitätsbibliothek in Halle* (1884). For this reason it has made some impact on the systematic catalogues of other university libraries. It is much to be regretted that the system of the Prussian State Library has never been described in print. Otherwise, owing to the fact that much labour has been bestowed on it by a staff of many excellent librarians, its importance for other libraries would have been greater, and trends towards a basic system for all university libraries would have been strengthened. Between the two world wars, much consideration was given to clarifying the theoretical bases of an ideal system of classification, the more so because the system of the Library of Congress and even the Universal Decimal Classification did not find favour in the eyes of German librarians: witness the fierce discussions about the merits of UDC during the twenties. Since not only great masses of books but many catalogues were destroyed during World War II, librarians had to act quickly after the catastrophe of 1945 to make the remainder of their stock and the new purchases available to the public, not only alphabetically but systematically.

Thus a number of university libraries, Hamburg State and University Library and Munich University Library among them, have developed new classification systems making use of the device of *Schlüsselung*, i.e. standardizing certain aspects or formal elements recurring either in the whole system or in special parts. In this way the order of certain formal elements is the same throughout the range of scientific subjects: historical treatments of a subject, periodicals in the field of the subject, bibliographies, handbooks, textbooks, etc. In the same way chronological sequence, regional or local sequence is the same through all subjects, whether in the main classes or sub-divisions. They are similar to formal elements and aspects dealt with by the auxiliary tables of the UDC. The classification system of the University Library in Munich, edited by Buzas, was published in 1957 and 1958.

A generation ago there was a trend among German librarians to develop an alphabetical subject entries catalogue (*Schlagwortkatalog*) as

G

the chief subject catalogue of a scholarly library. Many among them proclaimed it the subject catalogue of the future. The systematic catalogues of numerous libraries had not kept abreast of modern scientific developments. To many librarians they seemed hopelessly out of date and not amenable to reform. In such a situation, information for readers supplied by means of subject entries arranged alphabetically seemed to be an easier task than reforming antiquated systematic catalogues. But when the discussion was well under way, librarians recognized that the theory of the *Schlagwortkatalog* was not quite as free of problems as its adherents would make believe. The proper choice of a subject entry within a given field of knowledge presupposes an adequate idea of the systematic web of this field of knowledge otherwise the subject entries would stand isolated without proper relation to each other. On the other hand, every librarian knows that many students are accustomed to start their reading from a well defined point, expressed in German as *Schlagwort*. Moreover he finds encyclopedias and subject dictionaries arranged according to *Schlagworte*. Librarians feel quite prepared to cater for this kind of reader. They would like to build up a *Schlagwortkatalog* in addition to the systematic catalogue, if only they could find the time to do so. Only a few universities have been able to maintain two subject catalogues, a systematic one and an alphabetical one. Conditions being what they are, the most efficient thing to do seems to create a systematic catalogue with an alphabetical subject index that does not contain the individual titles under a given subject entry, but points to those loci of the system where books dealing with the subject entry may be found.

For some years past a new method of classification has been widely favoured by German librarians, because it proposes to combine the advantages of the systematic catalogue with those of the *Schlagwortkatalog*. This method has been devised by Hans Wilhelm Eppelsheimer. The systematic order of main classes, divisions and subdivisions, etc., is only carried to a certain point which varies according to the particular needs of a given field of knowledge. At this point instead of further systematization subject entries are arranged in alphabetical order. Eppelsheimer thus avoids the pit-falls inherent in too close a systematization of books and meets the demands of many students who cling to the linguistic term of a given subject. Moreover Eppelsheimer excludes from the systematic catalogue all titles containing a biographical or topographical name. He thus limits the systematic catalogue to books requiring genuine classification, relegating many books to his biographical and topographical catalogues. Some big university libraries are actually building up catalogues according to this method. Whereas the older systematic catalogues, in the wake of the Göttingen system, reflected the classification on the shelves, most libraries stock their new acquisitions according to the *numerus currens*, i.e. as they come into the library. This *numerus currens* saves shelving space. Moreover, classification on the shelves is no longer of as much use to research workers as it was some generations ago, when periodicals, nowadays the basic material for original research, were still few in number. In a library stacking its books without any attempt at even a loose classification, free access to the shelves has no longer any meaning. To make up for the closing of the stacks many libraries are planning arrangements for very large reference libraries freely accessible within the reading rooms.

German libraries are well aware that the systematic catalogue of the future must not be restricted to books, but should include those articles in periodicals that are important because of new facts or new methods, and contributions to *Festschriften* and symposia. The library committee of the *Deutsche Forschungsgemeinschaft* is at present engaged in finding out the best methods to cope with this problem.

The service department of a university library, dealing with the borrowing of books, accounts for a great deal of the routine work of libraries. German research workers and students are accustomed to taking books home for reading and study. It goes without saying that checking books going out of the library and being returned to it takes more time than checking books for use within the library's rooms. The continuous checking and recalling of overdue books alone takes a great deal of time. In addition to local loans there are loans to other libraries within the German library lending system by way of postal delivery. Some statistics will illuminate the actual state of affairs in the lending department of a big university library. Take libraries like those of Göttingen or Cologne. The lending departments have to cope with a turnover of from 200,000 to 250,000 books annually. As a borrower can keep books, with the exception of more recent volumes of periodicals, for four weeks, many books are permanently in active circulation, and in spite of the fact that he can apply for reservation of books, many a student is unable to get a book in time for his special study. To make up for this deficiency, some university libraries have recently built up so-called *Lehrbuchsammlungen*, i.e. collections of handbooks, textbooks, legal texts and commentaries in great demand, each item represented by a number of copies and to be borrowed within the rooms of the lending department with the least formality. There is every reason to doubt whether it is sound library policy to lend a normal modern book for four weeks to one person for home reading. But tradition is reinforced by the fact that opening hours in German libraries until recently have been restricted and reading space in the reading rooms altogether insufficient in relation to the number of actual and prospective readers.

Even German students would get accustomed to working in the library reading rooms if they were open late in the evening, at any rate in those university towns where students live near the university and its library. The planners of new library buildings will certainly consider this problem and arrange for its solution. Whereas Cologne university library at present can accommodate about 200 readers, the new library planned to be completed about 1965 will provide for about 600 readers. There is a marked tendency to discard the traditional big central reading rooms and to construct instead a number of special reading rooms with large reference libraries of the various branches of the sciences and the humanities centred around an information room containing a collection of general reference books, general bibliographies and dictionaries.

This is in Germany a period of intensive library planning. Not only were many older buildings destroyed during the last war but new universities have been founded, such as the Free University of Berlin, Mainz University, and Saarbrücken University, and a number of new foundations will soon follow. Berlin and Saarbrücken have modern library buildings. The new building of Bonn University Library, with its general reading room overlooking the Rhine, has just been completed. The new building of Stuttgart Technical University Library is nearing completion. Within the next five years new libraries will be constructed at Mainz, Cologne, Münster, Hanover, and Frankfurt. German librarians responsible for the new library buildings have carefully studied international developments in this field, especially library buildings in the United States. On the whole no startling experiments will be made. The idea of a stack tower, for example, favoured for some years past, is no longer cherished. The main task of the librarian will be to get the architect to grasp the functional requirements of a university library, the need to group the various departments according to their functional interdependence, and to arrange and equip reading and information rooms in such a manner as to secure for the research worker and student the maximum of practical comfort necessary for scholarly work.

11. RECENT DEVELOPMENTS AND FUTURE TRENDS WITHIN THE GERMAN LIBRARY SYSTEM

PROF. DR. RUDOLF JUCHHOFF

Bibliothekar-Lehrinstitut des Landes Nordrhein-Westfalen
Federal Republic of Germany

THE subject of my first lecture was the German university library as representing the typical scholarly library. I shall deal now, if in a somewhat cursory manner, with a type of library that has come to the foreground only since the turn of the century: the *Volkbücherei* (popular library), or *Öffentliche Bücherei*, as it is called now by many librarians, following English and American usage: public library. Whereas the university libraries and those of the technical universities and the regional state libraries, mostly old foundations established by the princes of the German federal states, are state owned libraries, the *Volksbüchereien* or *Öffentliche Büchereien* are the responsibility of the municipalities, large or small, or the rural communities. This statement does not imply that a given municipality must provide a library. There is no law to this effect. In fact, the elected representatives of most urban and rural administrative units, with the exception of the very smallest, have now voted for setting up a library; but this has been of their own free will.

The German *Volksbücherei* has been strongly influenced by the idea of educating the masses of the people. So the librarian has taken on the responsibility of guiding those readers not yet able to find their own way to the cultural inheritance of the nation, especially to *belles lettres* as the most genuine expression of the national spirit. Thus the librarian will advise his readers as to the choice of books to take home from the library. To be able to do this he must know a given reader's cultural and social background or try to get to know it, to learn what he has read up to now in order to make his borrower's reading a success. The responsibility is no easy one, and particularly difficult to fulfil during the daily routine work of the lending departments, as there is not the time necessary for a fruitful *Leihgespräch* (talk with a borrower on his reading interests, etc., as outlined above). But as a guiding principle of his professional activity it is ever in the librarian's mind; and it bears upon his professional training. He is expected to know the best part of the national literature and to be able to follow current literary production (translations of foreign literature included), and to select those books that may be of interest to his readers and valuable in furthering their literary education. This attitude, in the last analysis, is influenced by Friedrich Schiller's famous treatise on the aesthetic education of mankind. It was a grand idea, but it certainly does not cover the whole of man's experience. Other fields of human interests contribute to modern man's education: history and politics, economics, the sciences and technology. Modern democracy needs the educated citizen who is able to make full use of all kinds of information in order to get a balanced view of life around him and find his place in society. Education can no longer be confined to literature and the fine arts.

It follows from this that the librarian of the modern *Volksbücherei* has to select for the general reader not only *belles lettres* but books from the whole range of subjects in the cosmos of knowledge written in a style adapted to his needs. The selection of books from an overwhelming mass of publications is a task not easily performed. Only the *Volksbüchereien* of large cities, with a central library and dozens of branch libraries, have enough trained librarians to be able to assign the handling of bibliographical information and the selection of books in certain fields of knowledge to specialists. It is the custom for all librarians of a library system in a large city to meet once a week at the headquarters of the central library in order to go through newly published books and to give reasons for recommending or rejecting those books which have been assigned to them for reading and criticism. Thus, in many cases, book selection is a cooperative affair. It needs the librarian's concentrated effort, and although it is part of their official duties, and some hours each week are allotted for it, much of the librarians' leisure time also goes into it. The librarians of the smaller towns, besides using their own critical judgment, make use of the critiques of new books in general periodicals and of the short book reviews in the library periodical *Bücherei und Bildung* (published by the Verein Deutscher Volksbibliothekare, the professional association). They are as a rule very up to date and to a great extent written by specialists of the profession.

Volksbüchereien are there to attract readers and to ingrain the habit of reading in them. Going to the library to look up books in the reference department or to borrow books for home reading must not take too much of the citizen's time. In Germany, as in all countries with well developed urban library services, librarians insist that every citizen should live no further than a quarter of an hour's walk from a branch library; that the way to the library should be as easy as the way to the shops. Therefore the number of branch libraries should be related to the number of people living in a community. For example, in the big industrial town of Dortmund in North Rhine-Westphalia, there are at present twenty branch libraries connected with the central library in the centre of the city, where the book selection and cataloguing for the whole library system is done and a union catalogue of the holdings in all branch libraries is kept.

Much care is now being devoted to book departments for children and juveniles, i.e. for readers up to the ages of 14 and 18 respectively. In some cases there are even separate libraries for children and juveniles built according to the needs of this special type of library. They are run by librarians specializing in this kind of work. Interesting experiments are being made. To bring the leisure time of children and adolescents into purposeful connexion with their school life, libraries for children and juveniles are being placed in elementary and vocational schools in the same way that branch libraries for adult readers have been placed at the entrance to big industrial plants, or even within their precincts, thus bringing a man's or woman's workday life into purposeful relation with his or her spare time

Up to the last war, as a rule, readers could not choose freely among books, because the books were kept in stacks behind the lending desk and could be obtained only through the librarian. This, of course, gave him an opportunity of conversing with readers and giving advice on the choice of books. But open access to shelves (*Freihandbücherei*) in all rooms of the library is the standard practice now. Normally there is the division into poetry, drama and fiction on the one hand and *Sachliteratur* on the other. Whereas the arrangement of *belles lettres* on the shelves is alphabetical, that of *Sachliteratur* is in many libraries according to a system devised by a working party of librarians in the mid-fifties and published as *Allegemeine Systematik für Büchereien* (ASB). The *Freihandbücherei* is a boon for those readers—and their number is fast increasing—who are really interested in certain subjects either for their general education or for their vocational training and who, browsing among the books on the shelves, very soon learn to choose the right book for their special needs. Thus the *Freihandbücherei* has been a marked success. Even in this kind of library, of course, the librarian is still at the disposal of the reader who may wish to get his advice, and in accordance with his training the librarian will indeed wish to give such advice; but there is no longer a barrier between the reader and the books, and the librarian is no longer the unavoidable intermediary between the reader and the shelves, with all the delay and possible embarrassment for some readers that this system sometimes entailed.

The very small towns and the rural communities, as might be expected, do not have the means to support a library of their own, nor can they pay full-time trained librarians. Instead they have to be content with voluntary helpers, or part-time librarians, in most cases the village schoolmasters. To help these communities the various federal states have established special agencies, mostly attached to big municipal libraries but financed by the states, the so-called *Staatliche Büchereistellen*. The librarians working in these agencies try to get into contact with the village administrators and the voluntary helpers in the village library. They set up lists of books suited to the needs of the population in these small communities to choose from; they do the cataloguing and give all possible technical assistance. There is no coercion whatsoever: no community is bound to make use of the help offered by the *Büchereistelle*. But more and more communities are availing themselves of the services offered; and there is a strong incentive for the small community to set up a library: the state will pay half of the initial cost of a new library.

Most *Volksbüchereien* cooperate with other agencies for the spread of adult education, especially with the *Volkshochschulen* (University extension courses), where everybody is invited to attend lectures or follow courses in special subjects in the form of tutorial classes or discussion groups, being thus enabled to partake of the political or social problems of his time or to enjoy the profounder knowledge of literature and the arts. These lectures and classes cannot do without books. So the *Volksbibliothekare* have an opportunity of compiling special lists of books available in the library, or to display such books in special cases, with the invitation to borrow them from the library. Many a new reader has found his way to the local library through his membership of a study group of the *Volkshochschule*.

A characteristic of the German library system is the close cooperation between individual libraries of all types. The organizational pattern of this cooperation has been developed for some time past, but has never been so closely knit as nowadays. The cooperative efforts apply to the purchase of books and to lending between libraries.

As early as the turn of the century the then Prussian State, through the Ministry of Education, had allocated special funds to a number of university libraries for building up large collections of books in certain special fields. Under this scheme, for example, Göttingen University Library, already well supplied with books on Great Britain and English language and literature (due to the earlier political connexion of the Kingdom of Hanover with the British crown), received a grant to purchase all books dealing with any aspect of English and American civilization worth collecting. Bonn University had been the first to establish a chair for the Romance languages, before the middle of the nineteenth century, and had developed a brilliant tradition in this field. So Bonn University Library received special funds to acquire books covering the whole field of Romance philology. With this older scheme in mind, the *Deutsche Forschungsgemeinschaft* has since 1949 developed a comprehensive system of *Sondersammelgebiete*, i.e. of the literature of special branches of knowledge to be collected by individual libraries in such quantity that the library system as a whole is able to cover the world's output of all important scientific publications.

The *Deutsche Forschungsgemeinschaft* is a corporation representing all scientific bodies such as universities, scientific associations, etc. Although its finances are almost exclusively supplied by the federal government and the governments of the various federal states (there are smaller sums given by industrial and trade firms), the *Forschungsgemeinschaft* is a self-governing body independent of state interference. Within its general framework there has been set up a library committee of four professors and eight leading librarians to discuss all questions of library policy in relation to the needs of the learned world. In 1949 this library committee worked out the scheme of *Sondersammelgebiete*. Ninety of them have been assigned to about forty scholarly libraries, most of them university libraries and libraries of technical universities. The scheme aims at assuring access in Germany to at least one copy of any foreign publication (book or periodical) worth purchasing. The funds under this scheme are given by the *Forschungsgemeinschaft* with the proviso that the books and periodicals thus supplied must be available for loan to any other library for the use of research workers. The system has worked quite well for a decade. The funds allotted may be considerable in the case of a library responsible for a comprehensive special field of knowledge, such as the social sciences at Cologne University Library. With their own funds added to those supplied by the *Forschungsgemeinschaft*, the libraries with a *Sondersammelgebiet* have the financial resources necessary to buy all relevant books in their special field. In this way the forty libraries as a whole represent a universal library of modern research literature accessible to any person engaged in scholarly work. This applies notably to foreign periodicals giving the most up-to-date information about the latest trends in foreign research. About 7000 foreign learned periodicals in special fields are subscribed to by the *Forschungsgemeinschaft* and supplied to the libraries of the *Sondersammelgebiete*. They have been selected from a much larger number by a subcommittee of the library committee. The librarians on this subcommittee have had the help of learned specialists in the various fields. The list of these 7000 periodicals was published some years ago under the title: *Verzeichnis ausländischer Zeitschriften* (VAZ). This list is revised and supplemented from time to time.

As stated above, the *Forschungsgemeinschaft* supplies the funds on condition that the foreign books and periodicals purchased will be at the disposal of any research worker in any part of the country. To know exactly which library holds a certain foreign book is most useful to scholars and librarians; further, any librarian will be glad to know what books have been purchased by other libraries than his own, especially by those with a *Sondersammelgebiet*, because he may thereby be aided in his own book selection. It was these two considerations which led to the publication in 1951 of the *Zentralkatalog der ausländischen Literatur* (Union catalogue of foreign books), commonly called ZKA by librarians. It is published in monthly lists which give the titles of newly acquired books classified according to subject in 80 libraries. Thus every librarian can inform himself about the new books in history, medicine, technology, etc. About 22,000 titles are printed annually, and an annual index contains the titles in alphabetical order with additional locations of copies notified to the editor after the first publication of a title in a monthly list.

A list of foreign periodicals in German libraries, covering the period since 1939, is in course of publication. Five instalments covering the letters A and B are already out. This *Gesamtverzeichnis der ausländischen Zeitschriften und Serienwerke* (Union list of foreign periodicals and serial publications) known among librarians as GAZS is expected to have 40,000 entries including cross references. Several hundred libraries, among them hundreds of institutional and seminar libraries and the libraries of industrial and trade associations, have contributed to the list. It will be an easy matter for librarians and research workers in the future to know definitely whether a volume of a foreign periodical for a certain year since 1939 is among the holdings of a German library. Thus ZKA and GAZS are valuable instruments, as regards modern foreign publications, for the lending and borrowing of books within the framework of the well established organization known as *Deutscher Leihverkehr.*

Germany was perhaps the first country to organize the lending of books among libraries for the benefit of scholars by definite rules accepted by all libraries concerned. As early as 1893 an interlibrary loan service was established between the State Library in Berlin and the Prussian university libraries. In the course of the following decades this system was expanded to include all state-owned libraries and many others besides. But only in the years following World War I, when mutual aid became a necessity even in the world of books, was an all-German interlibrary loan system developed and the necessary formalities agreed on. The *Deutsche Leihverkehrsordnung* of 1924, revised in 1951, is the charter of the system. A major difference between 1924 and 1951 is the fact that nowadays also *Volksbüchereien*, provided they are administered by trained librarians, can partake of all the advantages of the interlibrary loan system. About 500 libraries of every description are cooperating in this way.

In principle, any reader admitted to an individual library can get any book in the stacks of any other library on loan for a certain period (as a rule for three or four weeks, bound volumes of recent periodicals for two weeks). Costs of packaging and mailing are paid for by the library that does the sending. The reader is only charged a nominal fee, about a third of a German mark. With the expansion of research in universities and industry and the need of many people in all walks of life to keep up with recent scientific developments, the interlibrary loan service has increased steadily. During 1959, for example, Cologne University Library sent 23,215 volumes to libraries all over Germany, and 10,804 volumes were received on loan for the benefit of readers in Cologne.

It would be a waste of time for a library, say, in south-western Germany to apply for a book from a library in the northern regions, if the desired book is on the shelves of a library in the south-west. To avoid this, the whole system has been subdivided into six regions. All application forms for books not in the local library ("red order forms") are sent to the libraries of the region likely to possess the book. Sometimes the first library approached may be able to supply the book, in other cases the book is obtained only at the second or third request, and occasionally there may be no copy of the book available. In this case the order form is forwarded to the so-called *Schlussbibliothek* (the end of the chain of libraries), i.e. the biggest library of the region which serves as intermediary to the libraries of the neighbouring region, where the same circuit is repeated if necessary. Of course, direct application to any library is possible, if published lists like the ZKA or individual library catalogues give a clue to the whereabouts of a required book. No regional boundaries are involved in such case.

On the whole this is a rather clumsy method and apt to delay the finding of a book. Under today's conditions of scientific work quick service is expected not only from the local library but from the interlibrary loan service as well. A book from even a distant library must be at the reader's disposal within a couple of days. A well-known means of achieving this result is the union catalogue. German librarians between 1910 and 1940 could rely on the wonderful bibliographical instrument known the world over as the *Gesamtkatalog*—originally a union catalogue of the contents of the Prussian State Library and ten Prussian university libraries, from 1930 onward expanded to cover all important German libraries. Publication of a list of titles of books published before 1930 had begun and at the outbreak of World War II fourteen volumes comprising the letter A and part of B had been printed. It proved to be a highly useful reference work giving, in its expanded form, locations of about a hundred libraries. But the manuscript card-catalogue, instead of being safe in a village in Pomerania where it had been evacuated in 1942, was lost, and all hope of a comprehensive national union catalogue had to be abandoned. Under post-war conditions in Germany there were cogent reasons to limit the scope of union catalogues in order to get practical results without waiting too long.

So the idea of building up regional union or central catalogues and making them instrumental in locating books within the regions of the interlibrary loan system gained the full support of German librarians and the state authorities responsible for financing the regional catalogues. Moreover, the federal structure of post-war Germany favoured the regional conception, as did the psychological consideration that cooperation among some dozen libraries within a medium-sized area, where most librarians are in lively personal contact, will work fairly smoothly, whereas the cooperation of hundreds of libraries with a distant central office is apt to suffer from all sorts of friction.

Of course there are drawbacks in this system of six or seven union catalogues: there is bound to be a certain amount of overlapping. But it has proved to be far less than is usually assumed. Although a comprehensive national union catalogue would doubtless save labour in the process of compilation as compared with the setting up of half a dozen regional union catalogues, there is the further task of continuing it.

Inserting title-cards in a very big catalogue produces new problems. The question of optimal size arises. All things considered, regional union catalogues of two to three million title-cards seem to German librarians the best solution. They correspond in size to the national union catalogues of smaller nations like the Dutch and the Swiss.

At various dates seven union catalogues have been begun in the German Federal Republic and in West Berlin. They are the financial responsibilities of the various *Länder*. Some are complete by now and have only to add the title-cards of new acquisitions. They have proved very useful as instruments of canalizing applications for book loans. There are union catalogues in West Berlin, Frankfurt, Göttingen, Hamburg, Cologne, Munich, and Stuttgart. As the *Deutsche Forschungsgemeinschaft* is naturally interested in the smooth working of the interlibrary loan service, it has contributed large sums recently in order to speed up work on those union catalogues still in progress. There is ground for hoping that all seven union catalogues will be completed in 1962. From that time the regional union catalogues will not only serve as centres of their own region but, taken together, will represent a national instrument for locating books and for giving bibliographical information to scholars and research workers all over Germany.

The function of a regional union catalogue may best be illustrated by the daily routine work at the headquarters of the most advanced of the seven catalogues, the *Zentralkatalog der Bibliotheken des Landes Nordrhein-Westfalen* in the University Library at Cologne. All applications for books not on the shelves of the local library and urgently needed for research are sent each day to the regional centre at Cologne, where the titles are looked up in the union catalogue. If the books are recorded there, the red application forms are sent to the library in possession of the books, which are then sent directly to the library that has applied for them. At present about 350 applications are received daily at the Cologne headquarters. About 70 per cent are dealt with successfully, i.e. they can be forwarded to the libraries on the shelves of which the books are available. This is a good result, considering that the union catalogue contains no less than about 2,200,000 entries. But the forty cooperating libraries are representative of all fields of knowledge. Besides the three university libraries and the library of the technical university at Aachen, there are a good many special libraries representing subjects ranging from theology to metallurgy. Applications for titles not to be found in the union catalogue at Cologne are forwarded to the union catalogue of Hesse at Frankfurt, where on the average a further 40 per cent are located. When all union catalogues are completed and functioning in accordance with expectations, those applications which cannot be dealt with satisfactorily at Frankfurt will go to the neighbouring union catalogue at Stuttgart, and so forth. Judging from the results of the present restricted cooperation between some of the union catalogues, it would seem fair to assume that, when the whole system is well established, only rarely will an application be returned without locating the book in a German library. Even if the book is found only at the last stage of the circuit of union catalogues it should not take more than 8 to 10 days for the reader to get the book.

The installation of modern apparatus, such as teleprinters, will further shorten the time between the first application at the local library and the delivery of a book from a library somewhere in Germany.

A new development in union cataloguing, restricted for the time being to the *Land* North Rhine-Westphalia, is worth mentioning. As stated before, *Volksbüchereien* are participating to a considerable extent in the interlibrary loan service. This causes a great drain on the book resources of the larger scholarly libraries, in particular the university libraries, especially as regard books in the German language. In the search for balance in mutual aid, the *Volksbüchereien* of the medium-sized and large towns have agreed on a scheme of subject specialization as regards German publications from 1956 onwards. Twenty libraries cooperate in purchasing all German books of any value in the same

12. BOOKS AND LIBRARIES IN OUR TIME IV:
CONCLUSION OF THE TURKISH SERIES

PROF. ETHELYN MARKLEY
University of Ankara

ONE of the purposes in convening the International Series of Lectures in Librarianship was to bring before librarians, friends of libraries, and students of librarianship in Turkey a body of information concerning library systems and problems in other countries. To help us accomplish this aim, leading members of the library profession in the United States, Great Britain, and Germany have come to Turkey to present descriptions and analyses of the structures of library organization in their countries. Still another country, Denmark, has sent its contribution to be translated and included in the published series.*

Here we have heard vivid accounts of the history of library growth, of the governmental regulations within which libraries operate, of the public support, both financial and moral, which they enjoy, and of the specialized services they are able to provide, such as publishing, adult education, and cultural programs, in addition to the traditional ones of collecting books and making them available for use. We have heard of the great variety of activities sponsored by librarians themselves; of their professional organizations, their cooperative projects, their struggle for professional status, of their continuous efforts to raise standards of library service and of library education, and something of the measure of their success.

The papers, as they have been presented, have constituted, in effect, a seminar in comparative librarianship. This is a most felicitous development, for comparative study is one of the more rewarding and economical methods of arriving at value judgments. By comparing problems, practices, and objectives, we are able to measure our standards of performance, diagnose our weaknesses, remedy our faults, and share our strength.

In addition to carrying out their traditional role as lenders, librarians have long been unabashed borrowers, openly and industriously picking each other's brains, turning others' experiences to their own advantage, and adapting techniques developed by other librarians to their own

* The English edition includes also a Canadian contribution not in the Turkish original.

uses. They have been just as eager to share as to borrow and they have diligently reported in the library press full accounts of their experiments, projects, ideas, reorganizations, building plans, devices, expedients, and schemes for improved service. Thus, there has accumulated over the years a pool of information about librarianship which is rightly considered the common property of all librarians. This is often referred to as the "literature" of librarianship, but it may be more accurately called the "material" of librarianship, analogous to the recognized body of music material that is the universal property of all musicians, freely available and adaptable to individual requirements.

Although the problems and material of librarianship are universal, the language, unlike that of music, is not. The composer's solution of a musical problem in mood or harmony can be heard or read in musical notation and immediately understood by a musician who speaks a different language. But the librarian's solution of his problem must be described and translated into several or many languages before it can become part of the universally available body of knowledge. This, in itself, constitutes one of our most serious professional problems.

Turkish librarians and students have been deprived of the use of much of the material of librarianship because by far the greatest part of it, particularly the modern literature, is in English and it has not been translated. We hope we have reduced some measure of this handicap through presenting here in translation the essential features of librarianship as it is practised in the countries represented by our visitors and our absent contributor. Each of them has made a contribution to Turkey, to increase the volume and to enrich the substance of our pool of available material in librarianship. It is free of copyright and customs restrictions and ready for us to use as we are able to adapt it to our needs.

We have gained much from the excursion into comparative librarianship. It has stimulated thought on our own library problems and the potentialities of a national system of library development. It has sharpened our sense of professional obligation; it has deepened our appreciation of the necessity of professional education; and it has brought us into close contact with some of the most perceptive thinkers and executives in the world of librarianship today. With such valuable precepts and examples to draw upon, our resources are indeed greatly increased.

The last lecture in the series adds the experiences of still another country to the pool of knowledge. Denmark is justly famous for its modern system of public libraries as well as for its special libraries. One of the most scholarly library periodicals, and one of the international character, *Libri*, is published in Copenhagen. Denmark's library school has been serving the profession for many years and its librarians have long been active in international professional associations.

Miss Elise Munch-Petersen, whose lecture on Danish library systems follows, became an Assistant Inspector of the State Inspection for Public Libraries in 1959. She graduated from the Danish Library School in 1956, joined the staff of the Copenhagen Public Library for a time, and then went to the Dragor Public Library where she was head librarian from 1956 to 1959. Miss Munch-Petersen has been a frequent contributor to Danish publications on librarianship.

13. THE PUBLIC LIBRARY SYSTEM OF DENMARK

ELISE MUNCH-PETERSEN

State Inspectorate for Public Libraries, Denmark

In order to form a true picture of the organization and functions of the Danish Public Library system it is necessary first of all to be quite clear about the framework within which it operates.

The Danish library system comprises two groups of libraries available to the public: the scientific or research libraries, and the public libraries. This division is a purely historical one since only in this century did the public libraries begin to develop a comprehensive library service in the modern sense, whereas the research libraries are in many cases direct descendants of old royal institutions.

When the public libraries were first formed there already existed a library system which guarded the interests of scholarly research and also functioned as a national library. In these circumstances the public libraries could develop a public service which had as its aim to contribute towards the general education of the people at all stages, to supplement the teaching of the schools and assist in the further education, training and self-development of the individual. Thus these two types of libraries differ from one another in the composition and nature of their holdings. But they are alike in that they are both open to the public and accessible to every member of the community. Generally speaking then, the policy of the research libraries is to purchase and make available learned and scientific works, and to fulfil the functions of a national library. There is copyright deposit of all Danish fiction, but this is only available for loan in exceptional cases for the purposes of study. Foreign fiction is available in the libraries of the humanistic faculties where it can be borrowed without restriction. The policy of the public libraries therefore is to provide popular non-fiction, Danish fiction and foreign fiction in the original language most in demand. These two types of libraries thus supplement one another and there is very close cooperation between them which will be described in more detail below.

THE PUBLIC LIBRARIES

The aim of Danish public libraries is set out in §1 in the Public Libraries Act. The Act goes on to state how the funds for running libraries shall be procured and sets out the conditions which libraries must satisfy in order to be sanctioned by the Act. The Act can be regarded as one authorizing subsidies, in that the libraries receive a subsidy from the state which is calculated on the basis of local grants to the individual libraries. This state subsidy gives the state the right to lay down by law a number of requirements which must be satisfied before a subsidy can be given. The amount of this state subsidy is computed by the State Inspection of Public Libraries which supervises the administration of libraries as well as giving them advice and guidance.

As a rule, public libraries are owned by the municipal authority but they can also be independent or owned by an association formed for the purposes of running a library. The general tendency, however, is to make all public libraries come under the municipal authority.

The original Public Libraries Act of 1920 has been revised several times, most recently in 1959. The Act begins with an objects clause:

1. The purpose of public libraries is to promote the general diffusion of knowledge and information by means of fiction and non fiction books which lead to the general development of culture. Such libraries may be awarded grants from the State and the municipalities in accordance with the provisions of this Act.

Thus in order to fulfil the requirements laid down by the Library Act public libraries must contain a stock of books which is as comprehensive and as unprejudiced as possible. All points of view must be represented, political, commercial, religious, and the library must make it possible for the general public to follow literary developments both at home and abroad. A public library for a limited group of the community belonging to a certain party or a particular religion is therefore out of the question since the library must be accessible to all in the district and must represent all points of view, those of the minority as well as the majority. Moreover the holdings shall be of a general educational nature; the fiction, for example, shall not be merely for light entertainment. Defined thus, the public library is a most important cultural factor, based on a broad democratic foundation with the books chosen on grounds of quality alone. Such a library is of invaluable importance for the culture of a people, for their development and their national sense of liberty and independence. And the ideal demands formulated in the objects clause quoted regards the Danish public library as the foundation upon which they rest.

The Public Libraries Act goes on to recommend that books may be borrowed free for home reading by all members of the community within the area in which the library operates. This means that children as well as adults are allowed to use the library. Many local authorities have started special children's libraries in addition to the ordinary libraries. They are run along the same lines and receive a subsidy from the state in the same way. Children's libraries under the same local authority form a single administrative unit. They work in close co-operation with the adult library and with the school and it is considered of enormous value that children get used to using a library at an early age, partly in connexion with their school lessons and partly in their spare time, so that they will continue the habit as a matter of course when they grow up.

Public libraries are not compulsory in Denmark, but the Public Libraries Act lays down that in districts where on the 1st April 1960 there is no recognized public library, the municipal council shall, if written request to that effect be made by a local library association supported by at least 10 per cent of the local population, take steps to see that within a year after receiving the request a library be founded which can be recognized under the Act.

The Public Libraries Act also covers libraries for those sections of the community which for some reason are prevented from using the normal public libraries. For example, the state grants a subsidy to the Seafarers' Library, which provides collections of books for the merchant and royal navies, and to the Central Library for Tuberculosis Patients,which lends out books to all those suffering from tuberculosis, either in hospitals or sanatoria or in their own homes.

This is an appropriate place to mention the extensive work the public libraries carry out in hospitals and mental homes, as well as the facilities offered to men doing their national service by local libraries in co-operation with the Armed Forces Welfare Service.

PUBLIC LIBRARY FINANCE

Local Grants

The Public Libraries Act lays down that a public library shall receive from the municipality a sum of money which together with other local grants and the subsidy given by the state is adequate for the maintenance of a library according to the Act.

In order to make clear how large a sum is regarded as adequate, the Ministry of Education has issued instructions regarding the economic and financial basis of public libraries. These instructions deal in detail with the economic and financial basis considered necessary for the various types of libraries with regard to maintenance of adequate premises, stock of books and salaries for the staff.

By local grants, on which in turn the state subsidy is calculated, are meant grants from municipal and county authorities. In addition to these there may be grants from a library association which has been formed for the purpose of supporting the library. The subscriptions to such an association are voluntary and do not give members any special privileges in using the library. Lastly there may be grants towards the running of the library from public bodies, societies, savings banks, and similar organizations.

If the library occupies premises free of rent, perhaps also with free light and heating, the value of these facilities is also regarded as a local grant, which is assessed according to fixed rules laid down by the Ministry of Education. The amount is naturally dependent upon the size and quality of the premises, and if the library occupies its own building it is estimated on the basis of the building costs. This sum must not, however, exceed the total local cash grants. This arrangement has encouraged the equipment of good library premises and buildings and resulted in a number of fine modern public libraries.

In connexion with this matter of library premises, it is a special feature of the Danish system that the Primary Education Act allows large subsidies for the establishment of school libraries in new schools being built. This has had particular importance in country districts and many excellent premises have been acquired which combine the functions of school library and public library. The value of such premises is also assessed, as mentioned above, and the existence of this type of library does much to forward the close cooperation between school and public library.

Another special type of library is represented by county libraries. Their function will be described in more detail in the section on inter-library cooperation. These county libraries are a number of municipal libraries in the larger towns which offer assistance to smaller libraries within the district. The Public Libraries Act lays down that such county libraries shall receive local grants not only from the urban but also from the county authorities. The size of the county grant is fixed by the County Council, according to the needs of the county library which naturally vary according to the size of the area it serves and the density of population.

State Subsidies

The public libraries are required to submit a report of their activities and expenditure each year and on this basis the state subsidy towards the running of each library is assessed according to the following rules:

To every public library the state grants a basic subsidy, estimated according to the total local grants. This basic subsidy comprises 80 per cent of amounts up to 25,000 kr. and 40 per cent of the local grants exceeding this amount.

County libraries are in addition given a further state subsidy to assist the work they do in surrounding districts. This subsidy is 5000 kr. for all county libraries + 0·50 kr. per inhabitant in municipalities with less than 15,000 inhabitants within the area of the county library, with the exception of the local municipality in which the county library is situated. County libraries which operate a book van service are allowed a state subsidy of up to 50 per cent of the transport costs. The amount granted by the state to the public libraries appears annually in the national budget, as well as a number of special grants which are made.

A sum corresponding to 5 per cent of the basic annual subsidy is paid into a fund which makes grants to Danish writers, or, if they die, to their widows and children under age, as a return for the use made of their books in the libraries.

A further special state grant is available to libraries which have opened branches at military establishments. This grant may be used for book buying, binding and cataloguing in such branches.

THE STATE INSPECTION FOR PUBLIC LIBRARIES

Assessment and distribution of the state subsidies are carried out by the State Inspection for Public Libraries, which comes under the Ministry of Education and is the central administrative authority of the library system. It is under the leadership of a director and not only offers advice and assistance to libraries but also supervises their activities. The State Director of Libraries is the chairman of The Library Council, which deals with questions of principal importance concerning public libraries. The Library Council has 14 members, representatives of the government, the urban and county authorities, the libraries, professional organizations and the research libraries.

RATIONALIZATION AND CENTRALIZATION

The Public Library Act authorizes the Minister of Education to withhold $2\frac{1}{2}$ per cent of the basic government grant, from which to meet the cost of undertakings related to the whole field of librarianship.

For this sum the Danish Bibliographical Office carries out a rationalization and standardization of work methods and materials and the consequent saving of labour enables the individual libraries to concentrate more on true library work. The Office carries out, for example, central cataloguing, and issues printed catalogue cards which make it possible for the holdings in all libraries to be arranged according to the same system. Closely connected with this work is another service the Bibliographical Office offers: the compilation and printing of the Danish National Bibliography, as well as similar bibliographical assistance which it gives the research libraries. In addition the Office issues a great number of printed catalogues of varying scope, standard catalogues and special lists, as well as the bulk of printed matter needed by the libraries. The Bibliographical Office also arranges for books to be bound centrally and offers basic collections of books to form the foundation of newly started libraries.

A Contact Service sees to it that the libraries keep in close touch with the public by issuing special publicity material in the form of posters, book lists, etc. which, either generally or in connexion with some particular event, remind the public of the libraries' existence. Thus it is possible to deal centrally with publicity problems which the individual libraries might not be able to manage on their own. This sum also finances an Information department of the State Inspection which has built up a central catalogue of the books acquired since 1900 by the research and specialized libraries. The catalogue greatly facilitates the lending of books from research libraries to public libraries.

The Information department forms therefore a most important link in that close cooperation which exists not only between the public libraries themselves but also between public libraries and research libraries and which is characteristic of the Danish library system.

THE COUNTY LIBRARIES

It was realized at an early stage in the development of the public library service that it would be necessary to build up libraries around the county libraries, a type of library which was inspired by the English County libraries, if any adequate service was to be given to the country as a whole and make libraries equally accessible to all.

With this end in view a number of libraries in the larger towns volunteered to act as county libraries. Besides serving the town in which they stand they also supplement and assist all the smaller libraries in their district. In this scheme there are 33 centres, each serving its particular district, and each working in organized cooperation on the one hand with the local public libraries and on the other with the research libraries. A county library must be recognized and its district fixed by the Ministry, just as the lending of books to libraries and individuals in its district and the technical assistance it gives to libraries must be free of charge. Book vans are used extensively in the work of county libraries. Another feature of their work is that in addition to the holdings they maintain for serving their home towns they must build up a supplementary stock of books for supplying to the surrounding districts. The latter comprises in particular older Danish literature, foreign fiction in the original and more special literature which the smaller libraries cannot be expected to buy for themselves. These county libraries form the backbone of the library system.

Crowning the county library system the State Library in Århus acts —in addition to its function as university library—as a national central library for the public libraries. It therefore buys, apart from the books essential to a university library, much foreign literature, particularly *haute vulgarization* and fiction, which are too specialized for the public libraries—or even the county libraries—to buy for themselves. The national central library also lends out Danish books which the smaller libraries cannot be expected to have.

COOPERATION BETWEEN PUBLIC AND RESEARCH LIBRARIES

It will be seen from the above that the principle on which the organization of the Danish library system rests is that each library works within its own more or less fixed framework and does not extend its activity beyond these limits. If a library is faced with a request which lies outside its scope it must either apply to the appropriate library or refer the borrower to the library. Thus the public libraries give one another mutual assistance besides receiving help from the research libraries by this stratification of literature.

This principle is based on the ideal that every book of any importance should be available to any person irrespective of where he lives and of which library possesses the book. Such an ideal can only be realized by the close cooperation between the various types of libraries which we have described above. Any request which cannot be met by the local library is forwarded to the county library, and from there to the national central library, which in turn sends it either to that research library which may be expected to possess it or to the Information department. In the latter case the Information department will carry out bibliographical research and get into contact with Danish or foreign libraries until the wanted book is tracked down and obtained. This cooperation extends not only to all the various types of libraries but also to the Public Records Office and provincial archives.

TRAINING OF LIBRARIANS

Librarians in Denmark receive their training at the School of Librarianship, a professional school similar to others maintained by the state. Both public and research librarians receive their professional training here. That for public librarians takes four years: six months' practical experience in a large public library, then six months' theoretical education at the library school, followed by a further two years in a library, and finally another year's study at the library school ending with a final examination.

PROFESSIONAL ORGANIZATION OF LIBRARIES

The Danish Library Association has a public libraries' and research libraries' section, as well as sections for public and research librarians. It deals with many professional matters and has over the years set up a number of committees to enquire into and safeguard library matters. In this respect, too, is emphasized the unity of the Danish library system.

THE PRESENT SITUATION IN DANISH LIBRARIES

A few statistics will briefly illustrate the situation as it is in 1960 and throw light on the results which have been achieved on the basis of the legislation and organization within which the libraries work.

There are 1300 municipalities in Denmark. Ninety-seven have no public library whatsoever, while 159 are only partly served, that is they may only have a children's library or share unsatisfactorily the library of another authority. That is 19·7 per cent of the municipalities are still in 1960 either partly or wholly without libraries. Seen in terms of population this means that 184,274 or 4·14 per cent of Denmark's 4,448,401 inhabitants are still without a satisfactory library service.

There are at present (1960) 1352 independent public libraries in the country, and 172 children's libraries. That is one library to about 3300 inhabitants, on average. If we compare the population figures with the number of municipalities it will be seen that many libraries are owned by communities smaller even than a parish (the smallest local authority which exists) and are therefore ineligible for grants under the Public Library Act. The existence of these very small library units can only be regarded as unfortunate and the authorities are keen on the idea of library unions between two or several municipalities which would make possible the establishment of more adequate and effective libraries. The very small libraries, for example, cannot afford to employ a professional librarian. It has therefore become a characteristic feature of the Danish library system that the small libraries in country districts are run by a local person who is interested in library work, often the local vicar or school teacher. This, of course, adds a strain of idealism to library work, but in general the result is an unfortunate and uneven discrepancy between libraries in the town and those in the country, since all the large urban libraries employ trained librarians.

The combined stock of books in public libraries is at present (1960)

6,544,365 volumes for adults and 3,212,264 for children, making
9,756,629 volumes in all, or 2·2 volumes per head of the population. In
the year 1959–60 17,757,289 volumes were borrowed by adults and
10,647,948 by children, that is 28,405,237 volumes in all, or an average
of 6·4 volumes per head of population. In 1960 there are 658,143 adult
registered borrowers, and 443,582 children, that is 1,101,725 borrowers
in all, or 24·8 per cent of the population.

In 1959–60 local grants amounting to 29,513,649 kr. were made to
public libraries, corresponding to 6·6 kr. per head of population. The
state grant for the same period was 15,735,135 kr. or 3·5 kr. per head of
population.

The total budget for 1959–60 was thus 45,248,784 kr. or 10·2 kr. per
head of population, These average amounts however must be taken with
some reservation as the local amounts, on which the state grant is
based, can vary from library to library from 1 kr. to over 10 kr. per head
of population. Again, it is usually the small libraries in country districts
which are worst off. Many of them receive quite insufficient local grants
because the communities they belong to are too small to support an
efficient library service.

There are, however, strong local traditions in Denmark which must
be overcome before each small community can be persuaded to give up
its own little library and instead combine with others to establish larger,
more rational and more effective public libraries.

It will be realized from the figures quoted above that there is still a
long way to go before Danish libraries reach the goal they have set
themselves and which is codified in the Public Libraries Act. The
libraries themselves are the first to admit this and continue to work
towards the common goal. In this work the libraries are strongly supported by the government, as confirmed by the Minister of Education
in his speech to the Danish Parliament in 1958, recommending the 1959
revision of the Public Libraries Act, which considerably augmented the
state subsidies to public libraries. The Minister said: "The importance
of the public libraries to Danish culture can hardly be overestimated.
It is our responsibility to give the libraries such working conditions that
they can continue and improve their work, which is everywhere so
greatly respected."

14. BOOKS AND LIBRARIES IN OUR TIME V: NATIONAL LEADERSHIP IN CANADIAN LIBRARIES DEVELOPMENT

CARL M. WHITE

CANADA's progress of recent years in library development has caught the imagination of observers beyond her borders. No other factor has contributed so much as the organization of the Canadian Library Association in 1946.

Canadian librarians have long and close associations with the American Library Association, but the need of an independent association was seen as far back as 1901. Nearly 300 librarians resolved at a meeting in 1927 to create a national association to further cooperation on all matters affecting the welfare of the library movement as a whole. More information was needed, so a survey was made of conditions. It was not an act of secession; the move had the official support of the American Library Association.

Three stubborn obstacles stood in the way of an independent library movement. Canada comprises an area of 3,851,809 square miles— larger than Australia or the United States. The population numbers less than 20,000,000; there are in all fewer than 1400 libraries or library systems; and both figures were smaller when the survey was made in 1930. The difference in interests and outlook of the people was as wide as their geographical spread. Second, libraries range from the University and Public libraries of urban Toronto, each with a large professional staff and more than a million volumes, to small, poorly supported "one-man" libraries in isolated districts. These differences in size among public and academic libraries were no greater than the way they together differed in purpose and program from highly specialized libraries serving business organizations and government agencies. To some, therefore, it appeared as if Canadian libraries had little in common except the name. A third obstacle lay in the fact that Canadian books were not even in one language.

Undaunted, the survey committee argued that Canadian librarians shared a common responsibility for defining and promoting a national library program. It recommended that they band together to achieve the following specific results:

Provision of books by one means or another for everyone in the Dominion;

Creation of a National Library to aid in building up, organizing, and making available library materials to serve the Canadian people;

Improved library legislation and increased public support for libraries;

Reduction of postal charges on library books as an aid to promoting ease of access;

A Canadian Association Library representative of all library interests, with a paid secretariat and adequate facilities for field work.

A Canadian Library Council Inc. was created in 1941 and the long-awaited Canadian Library Association followed the first year after World War II, in 1946. Canada resisted a normal impulse to ensure representation of geographical sections and types of library in selecting officers. The new Association, it was agreed, should be all-inclusive in membership, comprehensive in outlook, and selection of officers was based, first of all, on proven qualities of leadership. Membership was 765 to start with; it is now over 2000. Operating income, $11,600 the first year, nearly trebled in ten years. The secretariat increased in like proportion. An act of Parliament in 1953 established a National Library, with W. Kaye Lamb as Librarian. Progress was made on all of the specific recommendations of the survey committee of 1930 and the Association branched out by developing a publishing program, raising standards for library service and personnel, improving statistical services, strengthening national bibliography and bringing the case for library development to the attention of a wider public.

Of the features of Canada's library experience which hold interest for other countries, four are discussed in the following chapter, each by a librarian who has shared in giving the national library movement vitality. Peter Grossman of the Vancouver Public Library contributes the section on regional library development. A former President of the Canadian Library Association, he has directed three regional library programs, in the Vancouver Island Union Library, the Fraser Valley Union Library and the Provincial Library of Nova Scotia. Robert M. Hamilton, contributor of the section on public library legislation, is the 1962 President of the Canadian Library Association and on the staff of British Columbia School of Librarianship. He was elected President of the Canadian Library Research Foundation in 1960, is active in both general and special library work. Elizabeth H. Morton, who describes Canadian activities in the field of bibliography and reference, was formerly a member of the staff of the Toronto Public Library but is better known as Executive Director of the Canadian Library Association.

She is the only one who has held the post. Jean Thomson, who writes of the "Highroads to children's reading in Canada", is Head of the Boys and Girls Division of the Toronto Public Library, which is well known for its work with children and young people. She edited the third edition of this Library's standard work, *Books for Boys and Girls* as well as the supplement for 1953–58.

Canadian librarians look forward to accomplishments which have not been possible so far, but considerable gains have been made since World War II. The library situation as a whole is plastic enough that a general summary of library thought and practice should perhaps be deferred till a later date. This chapter accordingly sets for itself the more limited task of selecting representative areas which can be used to illustrate germinal lines of thought and effort that are being followed, mainly in developing public library service in Canada.

REGIONAL LIBRARIES

PETER GROSSMAN *Nova Scotia*

A "regional library" is a public library which provides service in a natural geographical area rather than a single governmental unit. It is public library service, pure and simple, and the term "regional" applies solely to the form of organization. From the point of view of a library user, there should be no difference between the service available from a regional library and that from a municipal or county system.

The first public libraries were, for the most part, operated on a basis of local, voluntary support. As municipal authorities gradually accepted responsibility for library service, the local aspect was retained and the quality of the service varied according to the size and the wealth of the community.

The inability of the smaller towns and villages to provide adequately for their public libraries gradually led, in the United Kingdom and the United States, to the adoption of the county as a more suitable library unit. In Canada, unfortunately, the solution was not so simple, as the pattern of municipal organization varied from province to province. Where counties existed, many were too small for good library service, while in provinces such as British Columbia there were no counties, but instead, an indiscriminate mixture of cities, towns, villages, district municipalities, school districts and unorganized territory, varying in size and ranging in population from a few hundreds to many thousands. The problem under these circumstances was to find a method whereby the various units in a natural geographical area could cooperate in providing reasonably good public library service for themselves.

The first direct attack on this problem was launched in 1927 when the Public Library Commission of British Columbia organized a thorough survey of public library conditions and needs in the Province. The first and most important recommendation to be made by the Survey Committee was that provision should be made for "a library district, created for the purpose, as a unit for rural library service". This recommendation was followed by three basic principles:

"(1) Centralization of administration is required for both economy and efficiency.

(2) Local distribution of books is essential for the frequent interchange of bookstock needed for satisfactory library service.

(3) Assistance of a trained librarian is necessary for effective book use."

These were the principles on which regional libraries were founded and they are identical with those which prompted the development of county libraries.

As a result of the survey in British Columbia, the Carnegie Corporation made a grant of $100,000 to establish a demonstration "region", and the lower Fraser Valley was selected for this purpose.

The demonstration was conducted by Dr. H. G. Stewart from 1930 to 1934, from which time the service was continued on a tax-supported basis by twenty of the twenty-four local authorities comprising the region. It is interesting to note that the four which dropped out voted later to be included, and that the region was still further extended to include additional adjacent territory. While the main purpose of the demonstration was to prove the practicability of a centrally administered service over a large region, not the least of the obstacles overcome was the passage of Provincial legislation permitting the formation of such a district.

As a direct result of this successful demonstration, other regional libraries were established in British Columbia, on Vancouver Island and in the Okanagan Valley. On the Atlantic coast a similar demonstration resulted in a regional system comprising the entire small Province of Prince Edward Island.

Although a good deal of interest was aroused by these developments, little progress was made elsewhere in Canada until after the war, when three more library systems, varying to some degree from the former pattern, were established in British Columbia with the Provincial Government participating through the Public Library Commission.

The succeeding years saw the Prince Albert Regional Library organized in Saskatchewan and four regional libraries serving almost half the population of the Province in Nova Scotia. In Newfoundland, still another variation of the regional plan brought library service to many of the scattered seacoast settlements. Even in Ontario, where the county is a more workable unit than in most other provinces, a regional system has been formed in the more sparsely settled northern part of the province. A type of regional service has been evolved in parts of Alberta, while the most recent developments have come in New Brunswick.

The problems of regional library service are those encountered by libraries everywhere outside of the large urban districts. Regional cooperation may reduce costs, provide a wider selection of books and more efficient service, but the limited availability of books, the lack of direct contact with trained librarians and the inability to provide good reference service are difficulties inherent in service to a scattered population.

A problem peculiar to the regional type of organization is that of securing the cooperation essential for efficient financing and service and, at the same time, for developing an interest and pride in the library as a local institution.

Regional libraries are now in operation in eight of the ten Canadian provinces, bringing service to many towns, villages and rural areas where it would be difficult or impossible to operate independent local libraries. The nature of the geography and population distribution in Canada makes it probable that this form of library organization will be adopted even more widely in the future.

CANADIAN PUBLIC LIBRARY LEGISLATION

ROBERT M. HAMILTON, *British Columbia*

Fifty years ago, Rudyard Kipling wrote, "The law in Canada exists and is administered, not as a surprise, a joke, a favour, a bribe, or a Wrestling Turk [!] exhibition, but as an integral part of the national character—no more to be talked about than one's trousers". The history of library legislation in Canada exemplifies only in a narrow sense the fact that the growth of public library legislation and libraries generally is an integral part of the national character. The whole truth is that public library legislation, having always been considered closely related to education, falls constitutionally within the authority of provincial governments and reflects provincial and not national characteristics. Canada has ten different provincial governments and ten different library laws and they are remarkable as much for their dissimilarities as for their similarities. The statutes which provide the main basis for public library service are not the work of a central government.

The first statute was passed in 1851 and applied to Ontario and

Quebec when they were still a single political area. This statute was "The Library Association and Mechanics' Institute Act" and was designed mainly to provide education for apprentices and laboring men by means of study classes and libraries. Membership in Mechanics' Institutes was not restricted, however, and included business and professional leaders of the community. Ontario and Quebec became separate provinces in 1867 and it is notable that Ontario soon adopted new and wider legislation—the Free Libraries Act of 1882. Library development in Ontario arose out of the Mechanics' Institutes, and growth since 1882 has been constant. In Quebec Province the old act of 1851 remained in force until the 1930s. The Institutes were never as popular in that province and there has been no similar public library tradition. It was not until 1958 that a new act was passed in Quebec and organization of public libraries other than in the already organized urban centers is now in its formative stages.

In the other provinces there has also been a diversity of development. British Columbia passed its Free Library Act in 1891. Saskatchewan and Alberta passed their Public Library Acts a year or two after they were formed as separate provinces in 1905, but the third prairie province, Manitoba, did not adopt its Public Library Act until 1948. The old Atlantic Coast provinces also passed their Acts in more modern times: New Brunswick in 1929, Newfoundland in 1935, Prince Edward Island in 1935 (repealed, 1936), and Nova Scotia in 1939. The Nova Scotia legislation is unique in that it is titled the Regional Libraries Act and it is indicative of recent trends that in that province a regional, rather than an urban, program of library development was adopted. This was the trend in British Columbia and Ontario before World War II and is now characteristic of most provincial library expansion. Amendments providing for regional development, going beyond city and county boundaries, have been numerous in recent years. This is not surprising, because the first regional library service in the world was the Fraser Valley Union Library of British Columbia begun in 1930.

In all provinces public libraries are financially supported to provide free use for juvenile and adult readers. Local taxation and provincial aid are the means of financial support everywhere except in Prince Edward Island and Newfoundland where there is no local taxation.

Two of the provinces, British Columbia and Quebec have Library Commissions, each consisting of both trained librarians and community leaders, and eight of the provinces have individual Directors, all professional librarians. Both Commissions and Directors are responsible for the active development of libraries and come under a Minister of Government. The Minister in eight of the provinces is the Minister of Education, and in two, Quebec and Alberta, the Provincial Secretary.

At the local level, public libraries are governed by boards of trustees who are chosen by the municipal governments, or by a combination of local government and educational authorities, to represent community interests. The one exception to this is in Prince Edward Island, where libraries are governed directly by the Department of Education.

In the past few years library legislation in Canada has been revised so frequently in order to keep pace with local changes that a future of progressive development appears certain.

CANADIAN REFERENCE WORK

ELIZABETH H. MORTON, *Ontario*

Public libraries in Canada either have special reference departments or carry reference books in their general collections. The reference work is very similar to that carried on in the United States, Great Britain, and other countries. The unique features of Canadian reference work are the Canadian collections and the various ways in which the libraries have cooperatively joined together to encourage the creation of needed works of reference about Canada.

The national bibliography, *Canadiana*, was formerly a publication of the Toronto Public Library but with the organization of the National Library this work became a monthly publication, with annual supplements, of the National Library of Canada. It is printed by the Queen's Printer, Hull, P.Q., and is obtainable for a small sum to libraries and interested individuals throughout the world.

The indexing of Canadian periodicals and the listing of documentary films under subject headings is carried on by the Canadian Library Association in a monthly publication with annual cumulations entitled the *Canadian Index to Periodicals and Documentary Films*. By early 1962 a twelve-year cumulation of 1948–59 will be off the press and will be a permanent record of Canadian opinion as expressed through the magazines indexed and through the documentary films of these important years. The need for an index to technical magazines has developed and at the present time this work is being carried on by the Toronto Public Library. It is hoped that a complete indexing service can be established at an early date and such a request was placed before the Royal Commission on Publications at its Public Hearings last December.

An encyclopedia on Canada has long been needed and through the requests of libraries with the cooperation of the Grolier Society, the *Encylopedia Canadiana* was published in 1957. This gives basic material about the country and can be kept up to date by using such works of reference as the *Canadian Almanac*, the *Canada Year Book*, *Canadian Parlia-*

I

mentary Guide, the Canadian *Who's Who*, the *Canadian Postal Guide* and similar works.

The need for a bio-bibliography of Canadian authors and artists was expressed by reference librarians in Canada, and a project set up by the Canadian Library Association has encouraged the publication of several outstanding works on Canadian art and Canadian literature. Research scholars have long urged the microfilming of Canada's early newspapers, since much of this material is scattered and incomplete. The Canadian Library Association's project, which microfilms Canadian newspapers of historical importance, has filmed over 150 Canadian newspapers and other rare Canadian materials. This has been of tremendous assistance in writing the regional histories and in collecting material for works of sociology and economics. Since the collections in even the largest Canadian public libraries are limited, the need for a system of interlibrary lending has been urgent. The National Library undertooks to microfilm all catalogues in Canada of the important collections and to establish a union catalogue in its reference department. This catalogue is not completely organized but it is already giving public service and proving of great assistance. Interlibrary loan forms to meet Canadian needs are printed by the Canadian Library Association once a year and there is great cooperation between all types of libraries—public, university, research, business, children's and school—for the interlibrary loan of books. Some of the research libraries will microfilm materials rather than lending it or will provide photographic copies. In this way the limited collections of Canada are used freely by the entire population.

When Canada was a pioneer country, the neighbourly cooperation by which barns and houses were built, fields ploughed and planted, coverlets quilted and yarn spun, was brought about by having a "bee". Besides accomplishing miracles of work, the "bee" included meals together, singing, dancing and story telling at the end of the day. This early practice has established a pattern of cooperation which is reflected in the ease with which the reference libraries of the second largest country in the world work together to make the most of their reference collections. This is assisted by the Post Office Department of Canada which sends all first-class mail by air and has an inexpensive library rate for the exchange of books.

HIGHROADS TO CHILDREN'S READING IN CANADA

JEAN THOMSON, *Ontario*

It is hard to believe that a hundred years ago Canadian children had hardly any books. Their lives were bounded by the little villages or towns in which they lived. They knew their own fragrant forests and their own rocky shores and some of them had heard songs and stories of strange lands far away. A few had books, most families had a Bible and there were old fashioned school readers, but *Little Women* had not been written, nor *Treasure Island*, nor *Huckleberry Finn*. The great railway that linked Eastern Canada with the West was still only a dream and the children of New Brunswick knew practically nothing of the pioneer children of the West.

Nowadays the railways join our shores, ships sail in a few days across the oceans to lands that were once months away, overhead great aeroplanes fly across land and sea like birds, telephone and radio and television bring us all together and today's news is heard everywhere in the world as soon as it happens. Today's children are different too. Like their great-grandfathers, they know a familiar city or forest or shore, but they are at home too in distant lands, in far-off times and among many strange friends. They are not bound by geography or history or finance because the children of today have books which lead them to explore new lands and new worlds and to open up frontiers that their grandfathers never dreamed of. "If I were on Everest," said a little Toronto boy the other day, "I'd know just what to do, for I've read all about it." "Look, there's Mike Mulligan and his steam shovel Mary Ann," shouted two small children on a streetcar, "we saw them in the library."

What sort of books are they interested in? Everything! For books meet a child at the level of his own interest and lead him off to explore a thousand new avenues. A ten-year-old boy wants to read all there is about jungles and natives and tigers ever since he started *The Jungle Book*. A little girl says, "That was a lovely story; I know a Finnish story nearly like it." "You know," said another, "the magic land of Narnia is more real to me than my own country." (And in case anyone should feel that he is shut up in a dream world the same small boy in a period of two or three months produced statistics about the opening dates for one fishing season for every fish in Ontario, went exhaustively into the great plagues that had ravaged humanity (with a view to becoming a doctor) and announced, "As far as I'm concerned the Roman legions are shot— there's nothing left that I don't know about them".)

These, of course, are urban children who use the public libraries of one of Canada's largest cities. They troop up the library stairs like the armies of an ancient invader demanding, "What will I feed my turtle?", "How can I make a soap box racer?", "What are some more good family stories?", "I *like* books about little girls in China", "I always have to bring one book of poetry to read to my sister", "Just princesses please; some people like stories of animals but *I* like princesses". Their tastes and interests are as varied as their personalities, and the libraries provide them with the material they need to grow and stretch.

Today in cities and towns across Canada, Canadian children are well served by libraries with trained librarians who select books and help children find those books which will fit their particular need. In most libraries, weekly story hours are held and some libraries use puppet shows or films as a means of introducing books. Larger centers have built branch libraries to serve a larger area and population.

Many centers have taken Public Library Service into the schools. For instance in Toronto, which has the largest library service in Canada, there are at present thirty elementary schools which have libraries administered by the public library, with a trained librarian on hand one or two days a week to help the children choose their books.

But what of those boys and girls whose lives lie outside these centers, in places where there are no libraries and in homes where there are still no books? They are not cut off from this vital contact, for the libraries follow them. At the Calgary Stampede, in the middle of the pageantry of Indians and cowboys, the Public Library has its float of Mother Goose characters. Up in the Peace River and along the Alaska Highway, children's books are delivered by bookmobile. The librarians set out on long trips from Dawson Creek, carrying with them sleeping bags and all the equipment necessary for a jaunt of hundreds of miles. Library books are dropped on a rocky island by a supply vessel and hoisted by aerial cable to the Triple Island lighthouse in British Columbia. In the isolated logging camps of British Columbia, children receive boxes of books from the British Columbia Public Library Commission. If they need a book for a specific school lesson they do not have to wait for the next box to arrive. They just write directly to the Open Shelf Library in Victoria and the books are sent to them by mail.

In pioneer days, even when there was a library, boys and girls had to walk weary miles to reach it; if they could not do this they had to go without books. Nowadays it is different: the libraries go to the borrowers. At The Hospital for Sick Children in Toronto, for instance, there is a library which brings books right to the beds of the little patients. As you lie with your broken leg up on a strange pulley you can read about "Curious George", the little monkey who broke his leg too, or if it was your appendix that came out you can boast with "Madeline" of your lovely scar. If you find the hospital walls confining you can fly away on a magic carpet like "The little lamp prince". There is a story hour too in the hospital library and anyone who is up can come, on stretchers, on crutches, in wheel chairs, to hear of Jack and the Beanstalk or the Indian tale of Nanabazoo.

It is not only a hospital cot that can keep a child away from his heritage of books. Young offenders in reform schools need the hope, the direction and the courage that a stirring book can bring. In the Borstal Institute in Vancouver there is a well stocked library for these young Canadians which will help to open the gates for them to real freedom.

Young Canadians are making good use of Public Library Service wherever it is available. According to recently released figures from the Dominion Bureau of Statistics, children from five to fourteen years of age and representing 20 per cent of the total population formed 41 per cent of the total registered borrowers, and borrowed 46 per cent of all books circulated in urban libraries and 62 per cent of all books circulated in regional libraries.

Statistics, however, never tell the whole story. It is only when one is able to watch this joyful enthusiasm for books among the children and to realize what this happy relationship with books will mean to them in later years, that one can appreciate what libraries across Canada are offering to the young.

INDEX

DATE DUE